Gremlin Trouble!

The Cursed Roald Dahl Film Disney Never Made

Jim Korkis

Theme Park Press
www.ThemeParkPress.com

Editor: Bob McLain
Layout: Artisanal Text

ISBN 979-8-89609-038-0
Printed in the United States of America

Theme Park Press | www.ThemeParkPress.com
Address queries to ben@themeparkpress.com

*To Bill Justice, whose talent and huge heart enriched the
lives of so many Disney fans, including myself.*

*He delighted in sketching Disney characters on paper plates and then fling-
ing those plates like Frisbees into the audience just to make people smile.
They were unsigned so that the people who caught them had to come
back up to Bill for a signature and so he could meet them personally.*

*When I asked him what Disney items he collected,
he smiled and said, "I collect friends."*

Contents

From Bill Justice's own copy of *The Gremlins* book came this hand-written inscription from Walt Disney underneath Bill's artwork. It was Bill's favorite treasure from his many years working at Disney.

Foreword

I always tell people that I was just a lucky fellow who was able to find a job he loved. For me, that job just happened to be working for a unique genius named Walt Disney. There was no one else ever like Walt Disney and there never will be.

I joined the Disney studio in 1937 and worked there for forty-two years as an animator on both the shorts and the features, special projects with my friends X. Atencio and T. Hee, and finally as an Imagineer programming audio-animatronics characters.

One of the projects I worked on that was never made was the story of the gremlins concocted by writer Roald Dahl during World War II. Walt gave me the chance to actually design some new Disney characters and a book was published in 1943 featuring my illustrations.

I worked long and hard on that animated feature but, for a number of reasons, Walt decided not to pursue the project, despite investing quite a bit of money in it that we really didn't have at that time.

One of the few mementos that I have kept over the decades from my time at Disney is *The Gremlins* book. In my copy, Walt wrote in his distinctive cursive style: "To Bill Justice—With my thanks and appreciation for a swell job. Sincerely, Walt Disney."

He was trying to tell me that it wasn't my fault that the film got shelved and that he was happy with the work I had done. When I look at it today, it still brings tears to my eyes that he took the time to do something like that.

When Walt Disney World opened in 1971, my job was to program the audio-animatronics figures in several of the attractions.

Out of boredom, I sketched Disney characters on my programming console.

Among the familiar characters like Donald Duck and Chip'n'Dale, it seemed appropriate given the problems we often had to include a few gremlins. I had to always explain to people who they were and that they were Disney characters.

I am glad that my friend Jim Korkis is writing a book about them so that people will know who they are.

I've known Jim since he lived in California and attended those Mouse Club and National Fantasy Fan Club conventions where I talked to fans. When I visited Walt Disney World, Jim was often my "opening act" when

I did shows at Give Kids the World. Jim would do comedy magic and make balloon animals to warm up the audience for me drawing Disney characters on a big easel.

Walt used to call "Stalky" Dahl the "chief greminologist" because he was the ultimate expert on the subject. I consider Jim a top greminologist as well. He has reminded me of so much that I had forgotten over the years as well as sharing information that I never knew.

It was great fun spending time with Jim at the Disney Institute where he is an animation instructor and talking about the "good old days" at Disney like the gremlins. I just hope gremlins don't decide to mess with his book to keep their secrets secret!

Bill Justice
Imagineer and Animator
March 1997

Bill Justice, who passed away in 2011, generously wrote this introduction, as well as one for a book on Jack Hannah that I was working on in 1997, in the hope that both would be published "soon." Twenty years later, both books are now published. We know better than to irk the gremlins by blaming them for the delay.

Introduction

When Walt Disney passed away in December 1966, his office at the Disney studio in Burbank, California, was closed off exactly as he left it, except for some activity by his secretaries in the first year who needed material located there and later by the maintenance staff that went in occasionally to dust and vacuum. It remained untouched until it was re-opened in 1971 for Disney archivist Dave Smith to document the room before things were removed.

Dave made some unexpected discoveries, including the original illustrated story script for the cartoon *Steamboat Willie* (1928) in the bottom drawer of Walt's desk. Another unexpected discovery was a plush doll in mint condition that Charlotte Clark had made in 1943 of the character of Gremlin Gus for an unmade Disney animation project. It had been in Walt's office as reference for well over two decades and no one had paid any attention to it being there. When Dark Horse Publishing created a new series of Disney gremlin merchandise in 2006, it used the doll found in Walt's office for its re-created Gremlin Gus plush doll.

Ever since I first heard about the Disney gremlins in an article entitled "Walt Disney and the Gremlins: An Unfinished Story" by my friend and former writing and business partner John Cawley in the magazine *American Classic Screen* (Spring 1980), I was fascinated. With that article began my decades of personal research into the seemingly cursed film beginning with quizzing John about all the material he uncovered but was unable to include in his article because of space limitations.

Over the years, I wrote several short articles about different aspects of the unmade film. In 1997, I interviewed Disney animator Bill Justice extensively about his participation in the film, since he was the one who worked closely with author Roald Dahl and came up with the final Disney designs for the characters. He had shared some stories in his own book, *Justice for Disney*, but I was able to prod some more information from his self-proclaimed failing memory.

I wrote a lengthy article showcasing some of this new research in 1997 for the never-published issue 11 of the Disney fanzine *Persistence of Vision* that was to be devoted to Disney during World War II.

I wrote an article over a decade ago that was over 10,000 words for the prestigious cartooning magazine *Hogan's Alley* #15 entitled "The Trouble with Gremlins: The True Story of a Never-Made Disney Animated Classic." For years, it remained the definitive article about the film.

Author and film historian Leonard Maltin used it as a reference for his introduction to the Dark Horse Publishing reprint of the 1943 Random House release of *The Gremlins* in 2006.

I connected with David Lesjak, an acknowledged authority on Disney during World War II, who shared with me information he had gathered during his own research into the topic.

Many people wanted a book about Disney's gremlins, but no one wanted to write it or felt they didn't have all the necessary information to write it. I decided to give it a try so that at least the material I had found could be used by others.

Gremlins remain an intriguing concept and certainly the Disney designs are loaded with appeal which is why people keep coming back to the idea of trying to revive the idea.

If you find any errors of any kind in this book, you must realize that I am completely blameless. It is the work of gremlins, and by reading their secrets in the following chapters you are now on their list as well.

Sorry about that. Be careful when you fly.

Jim Korkis
Disney Historian
November 2016

CHAPTER ONE

Walt Goes to War

December 2016 marked the 75th anniversary of the United States entering World War II.

Walt Disney was too young to enlist in World War I and ironically, too old to enlist in World War II. However, in both cases he found ways to serve his country.

Walt was hugely patriotic. He sincerely appreciated, respected, and supported those who served America and did what he could to help.

During a speech on February 22, 1963, when presented with the George Washington Medal of Honor from the Freedoms Foundation at Valley Forge, he said:

> Actually, if you could see close in my eyes, the American flag is waving in both of them, and up my spine is growing this red, white, and blue stripe. I'm very proud and very honored.

Just before World War II, the Disney studio was at the peak of its popularity, both financially and critically, and had relocated to a brand-new, expensive studio in Burbank, California. It was preparing for the release of multiple feature-length animated cartoons to capitalize on the unprecedented success of *Snow White and the Seven Dwarfs* (1937), a film that was still hugely popular even years after its première.

Disney films were distributed to fifty-five different countries. With the outbreak of war, many countries closed their doors to showing Disney films, which led to disappointing foreign revenue returns from releases like *Pinocchio* (1940) and *Fantasia* (1940), and the cessation of other planned feature films, including *Peter Pan* and *Cinderella*.

On December 8, 1941, one day after the attack on Pearl Harbor and the United States entering the war, five hundred anti-aircraft troops moved in to take residence at the Disney studio and would remain there for nearly eight months. Three million rounds of ammunition were stored in the parking lot.

The troops were there in case of a feared Japanese attack on the Pacific Coast and in particular to protect vital defense production plants like the nearby Lockheed Aircraft Corporation. Lockheed was expanding rapidly and many of its personnel were moved into offices at the Disney studio as well. The soundstage was used for working on military vehicles and anti-aircraft guns.

Walt said:

> They had fourteen trucks on this sound stage because they could close the stage and work in a blackout. That's where they were repairing all of the optical systems of the anti-aircraft guns. They had these guns all over the hills…because of the aircraft factories.

> They were sleeping in every room [at the studio]. I had to double my artists up in rooms so that an officer could have a place to sleep. They had their sleeping bags down on the floor. They set up their own mess kitchen.

Later that same day, at six o'clock in the evening, Walt received a call from the Bureau of Supplies and Accounts in the Naval Department to produce twenty training films on aircraft and warship identification. Each film was to run approximately a thousand feet. Instead of the hundreds of dollars per foot of film which was the standard price for a Disney short cartoon at the time, Walt agreed to do the films (known as the WEFT series, for Wings, Engine, Fuselage, and Tail, the four main points used to identify an unknown aircraft) for four dollars and fifty cents per foot.

The Disney studio committed to turning out three times its usual footage in the next six months. The Navy made the films available to naval bases and personnel at no cost, but gave the Disney studio a priority rating in obtaining the material needed to make them on an accelerated schedule.

The studio had already produced five war-related short films for the National Film Board of Canada, with topics from promoting the sales of war bonds to instructions on how to use an anti-tank rifle.

In addition, Walt had convinced Lockheed to allow him to make an employee instructional film for them entitled *Four Methods of Flush Riveting* as early as 1940, as he anticipated the need for such films. This film showed what the Disney studio could do with a technical subject.

The Navy was the Disney studio's biggest client throughout the war, but the success of the initial films being produced so quickly resulted in additional work from the Army Signal Corps, the Army Air Force, the Air Transport Command, and other service branches. The studio was given a confidential clearance and a top secret rating, as well as being formally classified as a war plant.

At the studio there were restricted access areas, special identification badges, armed guards, and even a U.S. Army searchlight battery unit set up in the animation building.

Walt Disney's identification badge is on display at the Walt Disney Family Museum in San Francisco. He donated blood to the Red Cross as well as writing a personal check to the organization for $7,300, among his other donations to the war effort.

Walt was even able to arrange draft deferments for some personnel at the studio because of the work they were doing and the cost and time of training others to take over that work. Their duties at the studio were more vital than other roles they might have been assigned if inducted.

The field of training films had been little explored before the war, but Disney developed them into an important tool that Walt intended to expand upon in peacetime. Some of the films were so effective that they were used for years after their completion. Unlike live action, animation rarely became outdated.

The films communicated the necessary information clearly and accurately. Animation could be used to show things that could never be easily seen in live action, like cut-away views of how a rivet enters the metal or what might be encountered in a specific strategic mission using top-secret reconnaissance reports as a reference to create the necessary models.

Shortly after the war, Walt stated:

> We learned a great deal during the war years when we were making instruction and technological films in which abstract and obscure things had to be made plain and quickly and exactly applicable to the men in the military services. These explorations and efficiencies of our cartoon medium must not be unused in today's entertainment.

Disney producer Bill Anderson remembered:

> There was a great pressure within the services of trying to get everything out. The Navy wanted their thing given priority. The Army wanted their thing. The Air Force had projects. The Marines had projects. So there was competition, and each branch of the service was fighting to get theirs done first.
>
> Walt was getting calls almost daily. "Can you handle this project? Can you do this for us?" and Walt would always say, "Hell, yes, we can do it for you. We'll find a way to do it."

Of course, the pressure at the studio was tremendous. Walt only charged the military for the actual cost of making the films, at no profit and no covered overhead costs, so it put a strain on the company's resources. Often these films were on a rush basis, with Walt giving a rough estimate over the phone, but even when that estimate was much too low, the government held him to that initial estimate.

By the end of 1942, the company had a total deficit of $1,216,909. Even under these "no-profit" terms, it was wise to get as many government contracts as possible because it kept the remaining staff at the Disney studio active, kept the name of Disney visible, and allowed for some experimentation that could be used once the war was over.

The studio didn't just do training films, but also made morale-boosting incentive shorts, educational films, and countless posters, insignias, and other artwork to support the war effort as well as troop entertainment. Walt even produced a short film for the Treasury Department with Donald Duck entitled *The New Spirit* (1942) that encouraged Americans to pay their taxes to help the war effort, since even the new, simplified income-tax forms were confusing.

Before the war, the studio's highest output in a year was 37,000 feet of film. From 1942–1943, it was conservatively estimated that the output was 204,000 feet. The camera department operated twenty hours a day (four hours a day were set aside for repairs and maintenance), six days a week.

The Disney studio had over one-third or approximately 165 of its employees (both men and women) actively serving in various branches of the armed forces. In addition, those employees still at the studio worked part time in volunteer positions, from serving as air-raid wardens and firemen to first-aid functions for the Red Cross. They also supplied on their own time illustrations for manuals, posters, maps, and other publications.

By 1943, roughly ninety-four percent of all footage produced at the Disney studio was done under government contract.

Eleven of the thirteen commercial entertainment shorts released that year by the studio featured topical references to the war in addition to the release of the war-oriented feature *Victory Through Air Power* that lost nearly half a million dollars and was never re-released because its content soon became irrelevant. Other animation studios got by with far less participation than the Disney studio and were not criticized for a lack of patriotism, so Walt could easily have done the same.

By 1944, over eighty percent of the revenue for the non-government Disney films was generated solely by the United States, Canada, and England (where the funds were "frozen" so that they could only be used in the country itself to help with rebuilding after the war).

However, even the storm clouds of war could not dim the unique humor of the Disney animators. As Disney producer Harry Tytle recounted:

> During the period when fear of Japanese bombing of the California coast was at its peak, someone suggested that, in order to spare the enemy the embarrassment of missing a nearby aircraft plant (and, incidentally, to save our own hides), we paint a sign on our studio roof, complete with the appropriate arrow—"'Lockheed, three miles *that* way!"

The gag was never shared with the military personnel, especially the highest-ranking ones who seemed to have little sense of humor.

Tytle also recalled that Walt wanted him to find out how the training films were being received by their intended audience. The studio had just completed a film on torpedo tactics for the Navy and Tytle found out it was being used at the naval base in San Diego.

Through the proper channels, Tytle requested permission for the director of the film and himself to visit one of the naval base classrooms to get a chance to gauge the audience reaction. He was informed in no uncertain terms that the film was classified and restricted, so it was impossible to arrange for civilians to view it, even if they had made it themselves.

In 1945, Disney was approached to do some of the famous SNAFU animated films that had been done by Warner Bros. As Harry Tytle remembered:

> Walt said we should have nothing to do with it. The reason was that the Army originally brought the SNAFU picture in to us. We made our best unit available to them and then they took the series somewhere else. We offered to do them for $20,000 apiece (half the going price for a short subject and well below our usual costs). Walt saw no reason why we should get into that again.

In his article "The Disney Studio at War," published in the January 1943 *Theatre Arts* magazine, Thornton Delehanty wrote:

> The government in Washington looks to [Walt Disney] more than it does to any other studio chief as a factor in building public morale, providing training and instruction to soldiers and sailors, and utilizing animated graphic art in expediting the intelligent mobilization of fighting men and civilians."

Walt never sought any credit for his many sacrifices. He always spent more than the limited budget allotted to him for his military productions in order to provide the highest quality that he could. It was just Walt's nature, but it placed the Disney studio in financial jeopardy and it took many years to recover.

Walt felt frustrated that the films had to be done so quickly and simply that he was unable to take the time to add his famous showmanship touches. He had to resort to limited animation techniques and other shortcuts, but he still managed to produce an outstanding product.

This was the environment at the Disney studio when Walt tried to make a feature film about gremlins.

CHAPTER TWO

What Are Gremlins?

The desire to blame mechanical or technological problems on something other than human error is part of our nature. The human mind yearns to have an explanation for things that are often inexplicable.

So gremlins were born.

Compared with other mythological creatures, gremlins are a fairly recent addition to folklore bestiary. They developed as machinery became more important and its malfunction became more of a major cause for concern.

For many people, machinery and technology have an aura of mystery and so gremlins must be responsible when stuff stopped working properly. These mishaps resulted, as they do today, in fear, frustration, and anger, and surely human error was not to blame.

Gremlins were generally depicted as looking somewhat humanoid but with elf- or goblin-like features, sometimes to the point of appearing reptilian with scales and claws. They were always of a diminutive size, most often a foot tall or less, so it was easy for them to go unnoticed and get into tiny places when causing mischief.

Reports of their appearance vary widely from glowing red eyes to grayish skin to completely hairless to huge sharp teeth and claws to being wispy and immaterial and almost everything else imaginable.

All reports agreed that they were able to withstand incredible temperature extremes, high altitudes, and violent winds, and had no problem adhering to the outside of a plane either through webbed hands and feet or clawed hands and feet or even more prosaically by the use of suction cups or hooks.

It is suspected that the concept of gremlins may have originated with the Germanic folklore of imps who were often portrayed as merely mischievous and perhaps a little malicious rather than outright evil because of their great delight in causing trouble for others at the most inopportune moments. They never directly attacked a human, but were masters of mayhem when it came to the devices that humans depended upon in their daily life.

The origin of the modern term "gremlin" is widely disputed, but is believed to derive from the Old English word "greme," which means "to vex or annoy." Some have also suggested that the Irish Gaelic word "gruaimin," meaning "an ill humored little fellow," might have been the inspiration.

The pilots of the Royal Air Force during World War II claimed that the name was inspired by a popular brand of beer favored by aviators called Fremlins.

Ralph Fremlin established his brewery in 1861 in the English town of Maidstone, in Kent. Fremlin's main product was a pale ale that became popular as public demand changed away from the dark porter-style beer. Branch offices were opened in London and other towns in southeast England to handle the demand, but the brewery was closed in 1972 and eventually turned into a mall. An elephant was the Fremlin trademark and company emblem, and appeared on all its labels and promotional material.

The implication was that imbibing too much Fremlins ale, either in celebration or to steady the nerves before a flight, would dull a pilot's senses somewhat, causing him to see things that weren't really there and to make errors in flight.

According to legend, gremlins were skilled craftsmen and mechanics who once helped humanity but felt betrayed. Now, they caused trouble and grief. Occasionally, there have been stories of gremlins helping pilots and tales of problems mysteriously being fixed once the plane landed and the gremlins had left. A heartfelt plea for help could elicit aid from a gremlin.

Gremlins were known to talk to pilots, sometimes encouraging them to act foolishly. In 1978, the crew of a Lufthansa jumbo jetliner claimed scratchy, garbled voices came to them out of nowhere offering instructions that helped them avoid a mid-air crash. Two years later, a British Airways pilot said a "strange voice" alerted him to a mechanical problem that would have proved disastrous had it been left unattended. Many similar incidents have been reported over the years.

One of the earliest mentions of the creatures can be traced back to the early 20th century, in a British newspaper called the *Spectator*:

> The old Royal Naval Air Service in 1917 and the newly constituted Royal Air Force in 1918 appear to have detected the existence of a horde of mysterious and malicious sprites whose whole purpose in life was...to bring about as many as possible of the inexplicable mishaps which, in those days as now, trouble an airman's life.

In 1923, a British pilot crashed his plane into sea. He later claimed in his official report that the accident had been caused by tiny creatures which had sabotaged the engine and messed around with the flight controls, crashing the plane.

This tale and others like it gained in popularity and British pilots began complaining of being harassed by gremlins, blaming them for such mishaps as engine failures, electrical malfunctions, bad landings or faulty landing gear, freak accidents, jammed radio frequencies, low gas levels (from the gremlins sucking it out of the tanks), cut wires and snapped cables, disabled carburetors, missing bolts or screws, holes in the fuselage, guns improperly firing, and missing maps and charts.

Gremlins were also seen sitting on the wings or nose of an aircraft or tampering with instruments on the plane in flight or sometimes making noises to distract the crew from their duties.

They were commonly reported throughout the Royal Air Force by pilots stationed in such far-flung places as Malta, the Middle East, and India, in addition to the more frequent reports in the air space over the United Kingdom and Germany.

Even famed American aviator Charles Lindbergh reported that during his historic flight over the Atlantic from New York to Paris in 1927 he found himself surrounded at one point by several vaporous, strange-looking beings in his cramped cabin and that they carried on an intelligent conversation with him about navigation and flight equipment.

Strangely, Lindbergh said that gremlins reassured him that he would remain safe and have a successful journey. He did not reveal this story until 1953 when he authored a best selling book entitled *The Spirit of St. Louis* about his trip:

> I saw them plain as day—transparent forms that moved freely about. They looked grim and menacing, but I never once felt frightened.

While there were reports during the 1920s and 1930s, the most intense alleged gremlin activity took place during World War II. The British Air Ministry did not assume that gremlins were merely a private joke among pilots but made some serious attempts to investigate, since there was often no logical explanation for some of the events.

The ministry even went as far as to have a service manual written up by a "gremlorist," Pilot Officer Percy Prune. It warned pilots that arrogance or over-confidence would attract the creatures and suggested ways to placate or distract them. Posters were produced warning against this imaginary enemy, perhaps in hopes of increasing caution and awareness.

Gremlins are mentioned extensively in the United States Air Force manuals published during World War II, including *Meet Joe "Flight" Gremlin*, a Training Aids Division Air Forces manual released in 1944.

Even today people have a fear of flying, but those early propeller planes of many decades ago did not give their pilots much reassurance of safety. In fact, most pilots were highly superstitious and carried rabbit's feet, four-leaf clovers, and other good luck charms, and even had nose art painted on their fuselage to try to ward off ill fortune. It was best not to tempt misfortune by ignoring even the possibility of gremlins.

German aircraft were also being plagued by similar problems and when American forces joined with the British, they also began to experience the same strange phenomenon. American pilots began extensively reporting seeing odd creatures fiddling with things on their aircraft once they were in the air.

The most logical explanation is that seeing little creatures that couldn't possibly be there was an effect of hypoxia from flying in unpressurized aircraft, with oxygen starvation added to cold, stress, fatigue, and other factors playing tricks on the brain and creating hallucinations, spurred by the stories of gremlins.

In his 1962 book *We Seven*, astronaunt John Glenn wrote:

> In the days of World War II, when combat planes were coming off the assembly line almost as fast as automobiles and there was a greater mathematical chance of malfunctions than there would normally be in peacetime flying, the flying fraternity blamed many of its technical problems on mythical little creatures called "gremlins."
>
> When a fuel line clogged or the control surfaces on an airplane got stuck for no apparent reason, the pilots and the mechanics alike would grumble that gremlins had gotten into the system and fouled it up. It was not always the gremlins' fault.
>
> Sometimes the blame rested on the mechanic, who had failed to check a part, or on the pilot himself, who had not taken enough time to look over his airplane before he took off. In a case like this, the gremlin was simply a convenient scapegoat.
>
> When the crews had done everything humanly possible to check their planes, however, and things still went wrong, the gremlins deserved some of the blame.

It would not have helped morale to accuse members of your own squadron or flight crew as having responsibility for mishaps. Yet, those who claimed to have seen gremlins and been the victim of their sabotage, just like those who have claimed to have had encounters with UFOs or Bigfoot, are adamant that gremlins are real.

Many air force veterans of World War II do not dismiss the concept of gremlins as merely a tall tale to relieve stress or explain incompetence. After the war, mentions of gremlins dropped dramatically, although pilots today still claim having encounters.

An article in the September 14, 1942, issue of *Time* magazine revealed:

Once, like all pixies, the gremlins lived in hollow banks beside rivers and deep pools. Then some of them moved to crags near the seashore and lived on pancakes made of yellow tide foam. Now they have moved into the air.

Last week, they were having the time of their lives flying all over the North Atlantic, Britain, and Germany in R.A.F. and U.S. planes. Usually gremlins are about a foot high. They wear soft, pointed suede shoes (occasionally spats), tight green breeches, red jackets with a ruffle at the neck and stocking caps or flat-topped tri-corn hats with a jaunty feather.

The September 7, 1942, issue of *Newsweek* re-emphasized their origin "as out of a beer bottle in the possession of a Scot" and labeled them as impish. By the end of the year, other well-known publications spotlighted the subject of gremlins, including *Life, The Christian Science Monitor, Collier's, The American Weekly*, and even *The Reader's Digest*.

Gremlins spread quickly from aviation to other fields. A sports writer spoke of them breaking up a duck hunting expedition. *Advertising Age*, in its December 7, 1942, listed the ways in which gremlins pester ad men. And a *New York Times* newspaper headline on December 19, 1942, announced: "Gremlins Bedevil Coffee Rationing."

Comedian Bob Hope joked that his 1941 book *They Got Me Covered* was ruined by gremlins. When questioned, Hope responded, "Didn't you read about the gremlins? Disney is going to make a movie out of them."

In the 1960s, the term "gremlin" came to mean a young trouble-making surfer on the West Coast.

Another variation is the femlin, a character used on the Party Jokes page of *Playboy* magazine and created by artist LeRoy Neiman in 1955. Publisher/editor Hugh Hefner decided the Party Jokes page needed a visual mascot. The name is a combination of the words "female" and "gremlin."

Femlins are portrayed as mischievous black-and-white female mischief makers, apparently ten to twelve inches tall, wearing only opera gloves, stockings, and heels. They are usually drawn interacting with various life-sized objects such as shoes, jewelry, and neckties.

An undated clipping from *The London Observer* newspaper in the files of the Disney archives is obviously from around 1942 and states that a gremlin "is an imp of bad luck to whom disasters are attributed in the roaring kingdom of the war-time sky."

In a press release to promote its upcoming 1943 *Gremlins* movie, Disney's film distributor RKO stated:

If he can ride the wings of your dive bomber tearing at 400 miles an hour toward a target; if he bores holes in your petrol tank and freezes your machine guns when you are about to bring a Nazi to bay; or if he uses your compass for a merry-go-round, then he's a gremlin.

It was Roald Dahl, author of *The Gremlins*, and Walt Disney who transformed the more horrible versions of gremlin mythology into a more appealing and friendly format, but for a variety of reasons the project they worked on together seemed cursed.

CHAPTER THREE

Who Was Roald Dahl?

Roald Dahl was born in Llandaff, Wales, on September 13, 1916, to Norwegian parents, Harald Dahl and Sofie Magdalene Hesselberg. Dahl was named after Roald Amundsen, the Norwegian who had been the first man to reach the South Pole just four years earlier.

During Dahl's lifetime he was a writer, a spy, an inventor, and a fighter pilot, among other credits. When he was young, his mother would entertain him and his three sisters by telling traditional Norwegian myths and legends in her native language. Dahl admitted that his writing was influenced by these tales.

At the age of three, he experienced the death of his older sister, Astri, and just weeks later, the death of his father. Some biographers have claimed that these events helped shape the darkness that was later reflected in his writing.

His mother sent him to several boarding schools. In 1929, he attended the prestigious Repton School in Derbyshire, the basis for many bizarre and memorable events that would later be recounted in his book, *Boy: Tales of Childhood* (1984).

It was at school that Dahl experienced the cruelty of children and teachers as well as the stupidity of unnecessary rules and the harsh consequences for not following them to the letter. Some of these indignities he saw and suffered were later the basis for events in his children's books.

Pupils at Repton were invited to do trial tastings of Cadbury chocolate bars, a memory that later helped inspire his book, *Charlie and the Chocolate Factory*.

Dahl's lust for travel took him to several foreign locations and eventually to East Africa, where he worked for the Shell Oil company until the outbreak of World War II. In November 1939, he became a pilot in the Royal Air Force at the age of twenty-three.

In September 1940, Dahl's Gloster Gladiator bi-plane crash-landed in the Libyan desert, fracturing his skull and breaking his nose. These injuries plagued him for the rest of his life.

He had been given inaccurate coordinates and gotten lost and low on fuel so had little other choice but to land his plane. He managed to drag himself away from the blazing wreckage. After six months recovering from his injuries, he returned to action, taking part in the Battle of Athens.

Later, after beginning to suffer headaches that would cause him to black out, he was reassigned as an assistant air attaché at the British Embassy in Washington, D.C.

It was at this time that he wrote *Gremlin Lore*, his first published book, and his second piece of published writing. The story was inspired in part by Dahl's love of Tolkien's *The Hobbit* which was also misidentified as a children's story because of its use of little creatures.

Dahl began work on the book in 1942, soon after his first paid piece of writing, "Shot Down Over Libya," was published in the August 1942 *Saturday Evening Post*. He had not been shot down but crash landed as the pilot and sole passenger in his plane, but he had previously been in air battles like the one told in the story.

He boasted that not one word of his story had been touched, but then later claimed that the error of his being shot down and the title had been his editor's doing. He later rewrote the story to be more accurate once he achieved some acclaim as an author. He received roughly one thousand dollars for the story, a remarkably high price for such a piece at the time.

Gremlin Lore was the length of a short story rather than a novel. He had written it to distract himself from the headaches he suffered.

In 1961, Dahl released the more lengthy *James and the Giant Peach*. It was marketed as a children's story and is generally referred to as his first children's book. Dahl would get irritated when interviewers gave the gremlin story that designation.

At this time, Dahl was using his post in America to supply intelligence information to Prime Minister Winston Churchill and William Stephenson (codename "Intrepid") who was working as part of MI6 and became a lifelong friend of Dahl's. Dahl's friend, author Ian Fleming, was doing similar work at the time.

Dahl would later go on to write the screenplays for the films based on Fleming's novels *You Only Live Twice* (1967) and *Chitty Chitty Bang Bang* (1968).

Fleming once wrote to Dahl: "My stuff is nothing, despicable stuff, but yours is literature." Fleming even provided the plot outline for Dahl's famous short story "Lamb to the Slaughter" (1953). Typically, Dahl was not as gracious in return to the creator of James Bond, denouncing the novel *You Only Live Twice* as the worst thing Fleming had ever written.

Along with Fleming, author Noel Coward, and others, Dahl worked for the British Security Coordination (BSC), a covert espionage network established in the spring of 1940 by Britain's MI6 intelligence service to spy on its greatest ally, the United States, and to convert American war isolationists to support the British fight against Hitler.

In one report that landed on Churchill's desk, Dahl had used his literacy exaggeration to claim that President Franklin D. Roosevelt was having an affair with a Norwegian crown princess. He was not, but Dahl loved gossip.

Dahl mentions in his essay "Lucky Break" that:

> My little *Gremlin* book caused something else quite extraordinary to happen to me in those wartime Washington days. Eleanor Roosevelt read it to her grandchildren in the White House and was apparently much taken with it. I was invited to dinner with her and the president. We had a splendid time and I was invited again.

This special access to FDR elicited significant information that Dahl forwarded to Churchill and Stephenson, as well as help foster the president's support for the British war effort.

Because of his injuries and their after-effects, Dahl was released from service in 1946. He was a confirmed flying ace on the basis of his known aerial victories, and it is estimated he had many more that were not properly recorded.

In 1953, Dahl married the American actress Patricia Neal, with whom he had five children. She came up with the nickname "Roald the Rotten" because Dahl was an accomplished womanizer, arrogant, callous, and generally unpleasant at times.

After their divorce thirty years later, he married Felicity "Liccy" (prounouced Lissy) Crosland, a much younger friend of Neal's with whom he had been having an eleven-year-long affair.

Crosland furthered Dahl's legacy through the foundation of Roald Dahl's Marvellous Children's Charity (a grant-giving charity to help children in the areas of literacy, neurology, and hematology) and the Roald Dahl Museum and Story Centre.

Dahl wrote screenplays for the James Bond feature film *You Only Live Twice* and the musical *Chitty Chitty Bang Bang*, as well as adult books such as *Kiss Kiss* and *My Uncle Oswald*. Among his best-known children's books, besides those already mentioned, are *Fantastic Mr. Fox*, *The BFG*, *The Witches*, and *Matilda*.

Dahl also had a successful simultanetous career as the writer of macabre adult short stories, usually with a dark sense of humour and a surprise ending. His short story collection *Tales of the Unexpected* was adapted to a successful television series that ran from 1979–1988.

In the November 8, 2009, issue of the *Guardian* newspaper, his widow Liccy Crosland said:

The sexiest seducer in Washington! But of course it was true. He was wildly attractive and handsome, in his RAF uniform, speaking in an English accent, a fighter pilot—completely seductive. And he was charming and intelligent. A lot of women fell for him.

People often ask me, "Did he tell lots of jokes?" No. It is in his writing, in his descriptions of things. It was a hidden, subversive humor, not a comedian telling jokes. Children were his friends; that's what kept him going. The fact that they loved his stories—that, to him, was a miracle. He said, "I feel a bit like a pop star."

He would make the most mundane thing seem fantastic because he would reinterpret it. He was always looking to help people and just make their day a little more interesting, because most people's days were very dull.

His granddaughter Sophie once described Dahl as "a very difficult man—very strong, very dominant…sort of roaring around the house with these very loud opinions." His widow claims that some of that behavior was due to the physical pain he often felt from his past injuries. Others have said that Dahl demonstrated that type of behavior whether he was in pain or not.

People are still debating whether Dahl was a heroic World War II veteran who started writing children's fantasies to entertain his own children and because he had run out of ideas for adult stories, or a conceited, condescending crank who delighted in tormenting others, bedded innumerable women and then cast them aside, and aired anti-Semtic opinions in interviews. Or was he some unusual hybrid of both?

Over seventy years after the publication of *The Gremlins*, Dahl's books continue to sell over one million copies every year. Whoever he really was, it is undeniable that he was a brilliant storyteller whose tales still enthrall today.

Roald Dahl died of a blood disease on November 23, 1990, at the age of 74. He was buried with his snooker cues, some very good burgundy, chocolates, HB pencils, and a power saw. Today, children continue to leave toys and flowers by his grave.

He once wrote, "Those who don't believe in magic will never find it."

Unlike some authors who had their work adapted by Disney, Dahl came away from the experience with positive feelings despite the *Gremlins* project never progressing to completion.

In his essay "Lucky Break," Dahl wrote:

Each day, I worked with the great Disney at his studio in Burbank, roughing out the storyline for the forthcoming film. I had a ball.

CHAPTER FOUR

Guide to Dahl's Gremlins

They don't tear stockings, wreck automobiles, and they aren't responsible for any accidents outside of the air. The only place Gremlins appear is in a plane and can only be seen by airmen.

—Roald Dahl quoted in Louella Parsons'
newspaper column, April 10, 1943

By the beginning of 1942, Flight Lieutenant Roald Dahl of the Royal Air Force had been relieved of active service as a pilot due to medical problems he had sustained from a plane crash near Alexandria, Egypt.

He was twenty five years old, six-foot six-inches tall, articulate, and given to a tendency of dramatic exaggeration and imagination in both his writing and general conversation that would eventually make him one of the most popular storytellers of all time with a host of memorable books to his credit.

He spent two weeks in a convoy that crossed the Atlantic Ocean on his way to his new assignment as an assistant air attache to the British Embassy in Washington, D.C. To help pass the time, he made friends with another RAF pilot, Douglas Bisgood, who was heading for Canada to be an instructor in an officer training unit.

Reportedly, the two pilots swapped stories about flying and gremlins. Bisgood would later contact the Disney studio when he heard of them making a film on the subject and an embarrassed Dahl would have to reluctantly verify that Bisgood knew quite a bit about gremlins before Dahl's manuscript was even conceived.

While, in 1942, Dahl was quite willing to make clear that the myth of gremlins was not his own invention but something familiar to the pilots of the RAF, it is interesting to note that as the years progressed, Dahl became more and more adamant that not just his story but the very concept of gremlins and how they acted were his original creation.

In the autobiographical essay "Lucky Break" that appears in his book *The Wonderful World of Henry Sugar* (1977), Dahl states:

> I also had a go at a story for children. It was called *The Gremlins* and this I believe was the first time the word had been used.

In a 1989 Australian radio interview, interviewer Terry Lane attempted to suggest that gremlins had been part of RAF lore before Dahl used them in his fiction. Dahl firmly corrected him that indeed it was Dahl who had put the creatures in that lore. In a 1984 interview with Disney historian Robin Allan, Dahl once again insisted, "I invented the name."

In fact, Dahl was well known for inventing new words,though never actually defining most of them, like lickswishy, figgled, whizzpopping, gobblefunk, snozzcumber, and frobskottle, figuring the reader would be able to come up with definition from the context of the sentence or the character's action.

Dahl would take spoonerisms and malapropisms and switch them around. He delighted in the sound of words and would rely on onomatopoeia.

He is credited with coining over two hundred words, including the term for the famous tiny people from Loompaland, the Oompa Loompas, who work in Willy Wonka's chocolate factory. Originally, he had considered calling them Whipple-Scrumpets.

Philosopher Isaiah Berlin, who knew Dahl well and understood that he could be inconsistent and subject to whims, was quoted in Jeremy Treglown's Dahl biography:

> [Dahl] initiated gremlins. That is to say, they were already there, in the Air Force, but he put them on the map. He was extremely conceited, saw himself as a creative artist of a high order, and therefore entitled to respect and very special treatment.

Looking at the facts, it is clear that gremlins and stories of their activities existed long before Dahl thought of using them in a story, and it is apparent that he must have heard many different stories from his fellow RAF pilots about them that he incorporated into his own version.

However, Dahl did create his own unique interpretation of gremlins.

For Dahl, the word "gremlin" refers to the entire species of these creatures, but specifically to the males who were all short and somewhat stout, with individual personalities but a common goal, similar to Disney's Seven Dwarfs.

A fifinella was an adult, female gremlin. Unlike their male counterparts, fifinellas were slender and stylish.

Widgets were baby gremlins who might appear male or female until they hit puberty, when their gender would become established. They were born in nests and since their forest home had been destroyed, Disney suggested that the nests were now in dark corners of airplanes. In his book, Dahl states that in each nest of thirteen widgets, only one will eventually turn into a fifinella.

In Dahl's original version for *Cosmopolitian* magazine, the female widgets were called flipperty-gibbets, but as the story continued to develop at the Disney studio, it was determined that there were too many new names, so all the baby gremlins were consolidated into widgets in subsequent versions.

Spandules were a breed of high-altitude gremlins to be found only above thirty-thousand feet. They lived in the rolling valleys of huge, white cumulus clouds, and all day they ate hailstones. They were at least three times as big as ordinary gremlins, with bodies specially designed for high-altitude work.

While mentioned in the book, spandules appeared primarily in the 1943 U.S. Army Air Forces Training manual, *Winter Draws On*.

This 26-page booklet was four inches by six inches and was illustrated by Disney artists in black and white with blue highlights throughout for the AAF Safety Education Division, Flight Control Command, and was used to teach pilots how to fly, maneuver, and land in winter conditions.

The artwork was actually done by an uncredited Bill Justice, with the illustrations copyrighted by Walt Disney Productions. In June 1943, Justice was assigned to draw spandules "for planned publication in a book for the Air Corps."

The front cover has a picture of a single-propeller airplane heading toward the reader with two spandules on the side, one of whom is blowing frost on a wing and the cockpit. The back cover has three spandules building a snowman that has a fighter pilot's helmet, a parachute, and a flying wings pin on the strap. The spandules were identified as the winter cousins of gremlins (who did not appear in the manual).

The spandule is similar in facial design to the other gremlins developed by the Disney studios, but there are also some significant differences. They have two curved horns coming out of the top of their head, making them look like small Vikings. They have big round noses and long white beards, and their bodies are covered with long hair. They apparently have no legs or feet, just trailing hair that bends like a tail. They wear big white gloves to distinguish their hands, which have long thin fingers and a thumb.

In the pamphlet, there are twenty reminders/warnings, one per page, and usually just a sentence or two in length, accompanied by a Disney cartoon. For instance:

- "Avoid icy and slushy spots when taxying. You may skid. Be easy with your brakes." The illustration is of a spandule pulling on the wheel, another spandule grabbing the first one's horns and pulling on him, and a third spandule blowing frosty breath on the spinning tire.

- "Make wide turns when you have ice. Steep turns with icy wings are suicide." The illustration is of a tipped wing covered with ice and three concerned spandules riding a sled that is quickly sliding down the wing.

- "Try all controls before taxying for a take-off. Ice may be binding a control-surface hinge." The illustration is of seven Spandules hanging on to each other's tails as they spin around the back tail rudder and blow frosty ice onto it.

According to the introduction in the manual:

In this book for the first time is pictured a close relative of the gremlin, the "spandule." These little fellows inhabit the air space above 30,000 feet except in the winter time, when they come down to lower altitudes and have been known to play around on the ground. Although not mean at heart, these little guys are forced by their very nature to do a lot of things to get a pilot in trouble.

Whenever an airplane enters their domain they pounce aboard. They like to test a guy out. If he is on his toes they probably won't bother him much, but if he looks sound asleep or a little thick between the ears, they are almost sure to plaster his wings with ice, load down his propeller, and do all sorts of tricks that can be real serious.

If you know where to look for spandules and if you keep a close watch for the first evidence of their handiwork, you can usually avoid a run-in with them. This book will help you do that. The life-like pictures of spandules which appear in this book were created by Walt Disney at the invitation of the Flight Control Command.

Woffledigits were only mentioned in the *Cosmopolitian* magazine version. A woffledigit looks like a wolf with six legs and all gremlins "firmly believe that Woffledigits feed on nothing but gremlins, but as a matter of fact they are quite harmless and won't touch anything but used motor oil."

On November 13, 1942, Walt received the following letter from L.A.C. Morton Smith:

Dear Mr. Walt Disney:

We of the No. 9 Squadron, No. 6 British Flying Training School, welcome the advent of the Gremlins to the screen. But Mr. Disney, sir, out of the kindness of your heart, for Christ's sake send us a Woffledigit. [The last word has been underlined in pencil by Walt Disney.] There is not even an I.T.S. over here [in Dahl's original story he created the concept of Initial Training School for gremlins to dissuade them from doing sabotage to planes], and although we are now [unreadable] plans for the formation of a large school, we are badly in need of a helper.

So, out of the goodness of your heart, could you send us a Woffledigit to [unreadable].

Yours sir, in spite of all unnamed Gremlins, Widgets and Glippiteygibbets,

M. Morton Smith

Roy Disney responded on November 23, 1942:

L.A.C. Morton M. Smith, #1396913
No. 6 BFTS
Onca City, Oklahoma

Dear L.A.C. Smith:

Many thanks for your letter of the 13th of November. Of course, you must have a Woffledigit if you think it will help you.

Please remember, though, that this animal, as its name implies, is apt to become "finger-in"; so keep it tied-up to the hangar door with a strong chain when you are not using it as a Gremlin frightener.

Sincerely yours,

Roy

At the bottom of the letter was this note: "A "Woffledigit sketch sent November 23, 1942."

CHAPTER FIVE

Disney's Fifinella

The word "fifinella" came from Fifinella (1913–1931), a British thorough-bred racehorse and broodmare who won both the Epsom Derby and the Epsom Oaks races in 1916, the year Dahl was born. Nicknamed the "flying filly," she rated the eighth best British-trained filly of the 20th century. So when Dahl thought of a female that flew, the name of the horse immediately came to mind.

During World War II, Disney's version of the fifinella was the patron saint of the Women Airforce Service Pilots (better known as WASP). In January 1943, the Disney studio provided a fifinella insignia for the group. Patches, letterhead, matchbook covers, stickers, decals, and even the WASP newsletter (appropriately titled *The Fifinella Gazette*) featured the insignia, which was shared by the 318th and 319th Army Air Force Flying Training Detachment.

Artwork for the character had appeared from Disney in an effort to copyright and trademark the design and it had caught the attention of some brave and talented women pilots.

The WASP was a a group of civilian female pilots between the ages of 18 and 34 who were employed to fly military aircraft under the supervision of the United States Army Air Forces during World War II. Their role included ferrying aircraft from factories to military bases, transporting cargo, testing newly overhauled planes, and towing drones and aerial targets for anti-aircraft practice.

At one point, 1,074 women had earned their wings and were the first women to fly American military aircraft. Using them for such duties freed up male pilots for combat service. The women all had prior flying experience and received the same instruction as male aviation cadets. However, they were not trained for combat and did not have gunnery training.

In 1943, the Women's Training Detachment and the Women's Auxiliary Ferrying Squadron were merged to create the WASP organization. The women were stationed at 120 air bases across the United States. During the war years, they delivered 12,650 aircraft of 78 different types. They paid for their own uniforms, lodging, and personal travel to and from home. And, of course, they were paid significantly less than their male counterparts.

Thirty-eight WASPs died during the war from accidents, and their families had to pay for their funerals. They were considered civil service employees and so did not receive military benefits and honors. They were not granted veteran status until after a hard fought battle in 1977.

Byrd Howell Granger, a member of WASP class 43-1, was the editor of the group's mimeographed newsletter, the *Fifinella Gazette*, which began publication on February 10, 1943, to improve morale.

In November 1942, Granger sent a request to Walt Disney, a connection made possible by her brother Frank Howell, asking permission to use Fifinella as the mascot for the WASPs.

This is the copy of the permission telegram from Walt Disney Productions' top legal executive, Gunther Lessing:

WALT DISNEY PRODUCTIONS

January 29, 1943

Miss Byrd Granger
c/o Fifinella Gazette-Army Forces
319 Flying Training Detachment
Municipal Airport
Houston, Texas

Dear Madam:

In compliance with your telegram of the 22nd. inst., we are sending you under separate cover design of insignia which we trust will meet with your approval.

You have permission to use this design and the name "Fifinella" as an insignia for the Womens Flying Training Detachment and you may also incorporate the same at your discretion in any issue of your *Fifinella Gazette* published at your station.

This permission shall be construed in the nature of a license from us to you in behalf of the 319th Flying Training Detachment. It is specifically provided, however, unless specifically agreed to by us in writing, this design and the name "Fifinella" must be confined to non-commercial and non-profit making purposes.

Of course, we shall be glad to cooperate with you in the event your detachment shall desire to use the design and name on stationary, pins and similar merchandise. Naturally, such use must be confined to your outfit unless we give you permission to the contrary.

Please be assured of our pleasure in cooperating with you and we trust that this little contribution on our part may be of assistance in building morale.

Yours very truly,
WALT DISNEY PRODUCTIONS
By Gunther R. Lessing
Vice-President

Granger later wrote:

Permission granted for two years to use without charge, the name and design of Fifinella. The cheers which greeted the [news] when it was announced at mess are an indication of the group's thanks to Mr. Disney and his staff.

Walt had a crew of five artists under the supervision of artist Hank Porter who did most of the over 1200 designs. Since Bill Justice was part of that crew and was the designer of the gremlins, it may be assumed that he was the one who came up with the fifinella insignia.

The original design had the smiling winged figure coming in for a landing with a red circle in the background; she is portrayed with curled horns, a yellow flight cap with goggles, a red top, yellow slacks, long black gloves, and red high-top boots.

The official permission was printed in the first issue of the newsletter, but the female pilots had already started creating homemade patches featuring the character. Some were leather, some were cloth, and they were worn on WASP flight jackets. Since these patches were homemade and never commercially produced, there were many different variations from the official design.

Thanks to the research of David Lesjak, who specializes in World War II-era Disney, I was able to find this account, written by former WASP Shutsy-Reynolds:

Fifinella was worn while in training...on A-2 jackets and on the white blouse. The patch was not available commercially.

They were handmade by both trainees and instructors. To get a patch made at Sweetwater [Texas Avenger Air Field], we made our own. I remember buying a large side of leather and with lacquer from the field paint shop made up about 50 which I sold. Money was always in short supply and the venture made for a fine weekend.

During the war, not only patches but letterheads, matchbook covers, stickers, decals, and other items featured the fifinella mascot.

In the second issue of the *Fifinella Gazette* (March 1, 1943), Jacqueline Cochran wrote an essay entitled "Origin of the Fifinellas" that was not approved by either Walt Disney or Roald Dahl, but gives some insight into these female pilots' view of fifinellas.

Cochran was a well-known and respected pioneer in aviation and was the director of the WASPs and responsible for their formation. She oversaw the training of hundreds of women pilots at Avenger Air Field in Sweetwater, Texas. Here is her essay:

> There is a fallacy going the rounds that the fifinellas have taken to riding the air waves only recently. I knew their mother well. In fact, I think it was their grandmother, for one generation could not make such a change in any species.
>
> Where the intermediate generation has been, is a mystery, but I'm sure they have been hiding out in some center of fashion and culture to ring the evident present-day results.
>
> I first met up with that irascible and dangerous female Gremlin over the Rocky Mountains in 1932. She pulled my compass off by some forty-five degrees and held it there until I was about to crash-land. She practically trailed me from then on, until the Fall of 1936, when she disappeared from sight. In the London-Australia race in 1934, she changed the signs of my fuel controls from "off" to "on," locked my cockpit hood so I could not get it open, and froze the flaps so as to give me a hair-raising landing. Thenceforth, I called her "Lady Borzia" and I suspected on that day that she had obtained help, although I never saw a Gremlin until some time later, and then only sketchily.
>
> In fact, I suspect that the meeting between Lady Borzia and the Gremlin, which blossomed into romance and gave the harvest of Fifinellas, occurred in 1936, right in my Northrup plane before my very eyes. I can't be sure because these mystic creatures have a Chameleon-like quality of changing their color to make the background a perfect camouflage. Lady Borzia had started a fire in my ship, the week before, while I was 16,000 feet up, but definitely it was without malice, for she allowed me to get down safely.
>
> Then, on this particular day, I noticed her hanging over a wingtip, gathering colors from a passing rainbow and storing them in what looked to me to be a cosmetics kit. Constantly, she glanced towards the cockpit with a coy "come-hither" look which caused me to suspect additional company and trouble. Suddenly, while approaching for a landing, the engine quit and the flaps froze and a few seconds later when I picked myself up from the pieces of what was once a plane, I momentarily noticed Borzia and a very handsome-looking Gremlin dancing off across the field together. He was certainly a Gremlin of

the finer type, for the Fifinellas have many rare qualities that could not have been inherited on their mother's side.

I look for the Fifinellas to be a good influence on the whole. I somehow feel that they symbolize a change in convention, just as the Fifinellas are a change in the Gremlin species, and to help rather than hinder their excursions into the blue. They will have their moments, it is true, but it is evident that they will not try to be just Gremlins or try to do the ordinary things that Gremlins usually do. They will be themselves, and I am convinced will even, on occasion, by their example shame the more abandoned Gremlins into better habits. These new folk of the air waves are certainly with us to stay. And, incidentally, they can be bribed. I've noticed they are particularly fond of applesauce, and for a whiff of perfume, the Fifinellas will practically do your navigating for you.

In that same issue, Granger wrote:

> The original deisgn of Fifi arrived in time to become part of the mast-head...the...issue also contained a surprise for the girls, for as a slip-in, we had inserted color repro's of our emblem.

That color insert also appeared in *The Log Book* pamphlet for the 319th AAFFTD (Army Air Forces Flying Training Division) in Houston, Texas, along with the following text:

> Members of 43-W-2 will recall that in their early days at Houston a warning was posted that all students must carry used postage stamps to feed and pacify "Them Gremlins." Not long thereafter female Gremlins, or Fifinellas, were seen shoving ships off the runways into tenacious Texas mud. However, no male or female Gremlins were seen in the air.
>
> The first student to see a Fifinella on board in flight was Sidney Miller whose phenomenal practically on-the-back spin recovery during a check ride was definitely due to three Fifinellas visibly (1) swinging on the throttle (2) holding the stick firmly forward (3) throwing dust into the Lt.'s eyes so he failed to note the goings-on.
>
> Those familiar with Them Gremlins will recognize that something new has been added. Formerly only Gremlins and male children, or Widgets, rode the airwaves, it being claimed that the diminutive Fifinellas lacked the ability to undertake such hazardous Gremlintrix as (1) playing see-saw on the artificial horizon (2) using the compass as a merry-go-round (3) drinking gasoline (4) sliding down the beam and rolling up the runway, thus making planes undershoot.
>
> Like members of the 318th, Fifinellas needed only training in order to turn in a good job. When the 319th was formed, a squadron of

pioneering Fifinellas arrived with the first Gremlins, forcing Them to undertake specialists jobs such as that of the big-stomached Puff Gremlin who sucks air from under a plane, making it jounce.

At Houston, Gremlins and Fifinellas are breeding at a rate sufficient to supply each cubstaff flier with a Flipperty-Gibbet, or young Fifinella, which reaches Fifineallahood upon the student's graduation to PIs. For the benefit of those students who have not been adopted to date (by the way, Them Gremlins take the name of their pilot, as Fifinella Richards) we present left, the best Fifinella to arrive at the Houston Municpal. Fifinellas are about a foot high. Whereas Gremlins have stubby horns, those Them Fifinellas are delicate and curled.

Them Gremlins have come a long way from their original homes of a 1000 years ago in the quiet shadows of river pools, thence to the mountain crags and finally taking to the air. Now Them have taken another step. Them Fifinellas, like the gals of the 319th, are taking the air.

Watch out fellas! They're dillies!

It is a grave social error to refer to Gremlins as anything but Them.

One B-17G Flying Fortress, *Fifinella* (Serial #42-107030), of the 91st Bomb Group, was named after the female gremlin mascot. *Fifinella* was lost on August 13, 1944, on a bombing raid of a railway bridge at Le Manoir, France, when it took flak and a fire started in the plane. It had flown fifty-four missions.

In April 1944, airman Tony Starcer, famed for his paintings on planes, drew a "nose design" painting of the fifinella based on the patches worn by the WASPs. A large bomb was added so that it looked like the character was dressed in a red coat and purple trousers, and was sitting astride the bomb rather than just leaping from the sky. The dark blue Starcer circle around the image added extra impact.

During the Korean War, there was also a B-29 Superfortress (Serial #42-6569) of the 19th Bomb Group named *Fifinella*.

The WASP were officially disbanded by December 20, 1944, as being no longer neccessary. All records of the WASPs were classified and sealed for 35 years, so their contributions to the war effort were little known and inaccessible.

On July 1, 2009, President Barack Obama and the United States Congress awarded the WASP organization the Congressional Gold Medal. Roughly 300 surviving WASPs were able to personally receive the honor with the rest going to family members.

In December 1944, Gunther Lessing sent another telegram to the WASPs:

This will serve as your authorization to use the name and insignia of Fifinella in connection with the post inactivation organization of the WASPs which is tentatively titled the Order of Fifinella. The name and insignie may not be used for commercial purposes or in connection with any merchandising endeavors from which profit is derived without our specific permission in writing. Also, you will be obligated to append copyright notice to all publications.

Walt deems it an honor to be numbered among your members with the understanding that because of his many commitments he will be unable to take advice or assume any obligations unless specifically agreed to in each instance. I trust you will understand the valid reasons for these reservations.

We regret your organizations' inactivation but you are entitled to rest on your laurels with the consciousness of a wonderful work wonderfully and efficiently performed during times of great stress.

Today, Dark Horse Publishing is attempting to revive Disney's gremlins and has produced some merchandise featuring the lovely fifinellas.

CHAPTER SIX

Disney Gets The Gremlins

Within months of his arrival in Washington, Dahl had written his first book entitled at the time *Gremlin Lore*. As a serving officer he was required to submit for approval everything he wrote to the British Information Services (BIS) based in New York.

He sent the rough draft manuscript to Sidney Bernstein at BIS. Before the war, Bernstein had been a British film entrepreneur who built many movie theater palaces and would later found Granada Television in England.

On July 1, 1942, Bernstein, sensing a project with fanciful similarities to Disney's animated feature films, sent the draft to Walt Disney. He included a brief note that stated:

> Flight Lieutenant Ronald [sic] Dahl has written a story about a New Dream Community that has risen in the Air Force, and I am enclosing you his effort which has been submitted through literary agent to a magazine.

> The idea, I think, has great possibilities, as a film, if done in your own inimitable style. I have no personal interest in the matter, and if you would be interested in communicating with Dahl, his address is the British Embassy, Washington. I hope to be in Hollywood during August and have the pleasure of meeting you again.

By the beginning of 1942, the Disney studio was having both financial and creative challenges. The closure of the foreign market for American films and Walt's agreement to make military and government training films "without profit" (only the cost of actual production) for the war effort resulted in a deficit of over a million dollars.

Money was going out but little if any was coming back in, and many of Walt's most talented and dependable artists were serving in the armed forces or were in danger of being drafted soon.

After years of experimentation and artistic growth, Walt and his staff were now feeling constrained by the restrictions of limited animation, technical jargon, unrealistic deadlines, and interference by military advisors. Because of time, labor, and expense, more creative options such as the developing of a new animated feature had been shelved for the duration of the war, although a small handful of commercial entertainment animated shorts were still being made.

When Walt received the *Gremlin Lore* manuscript, he supposedly saw an opportunity to do a feature that would allow his staff to utilize the military expertise they had developed, maintain their commitment to the war effort, explore Walt's recent fascination with the possibilities of aviation, and perhaps recapture some of the financial and creative rewards of *Snow White and the Seven Dwarfs* (1937) with characters that had some superficial similarities to the dwarfs.

It would be a wartime fairy tale and seemed ideal for Disney's animation expertise and talent. In addition, it would have the cache of being from a well-known decorated RAF pilot.

Walt immediately cabled both Dahl and Bernstein on July 13, 1942, to inform them of his interest. The telegram to Dahl stated:

> Sidney Bernstein has sent me your story of the Gremlins. Believe it has possibilities. Would be interested in seeing your material and will have our Mr. Feitel in Washington contact you regarding same.

Chester D. Feitel was a sales representative for the Disney studio assisting marketing executive Kay Kamen with merchandising. He was based in Washington, D.C., and so geographically had easy access to Dahl.

That same day, Walt cabled Bernstein his thanks for locating the story:

> Gremlins idea has great possibilities. Am contacting Dahl in Washington. Hope we will be able to work out something so we can produce it. Many thanks for sending it on to me. Looking forward to seeing you in Hollywood in August. Kindest regards, Walt Disney.

Three days later, Feitel's written report of his meeting with Dahl was being read by Walt and Roy in Burbank, California:

> Dahl is a young fellow...does not regard himself as a professional writer.... *Gremlin Lore* has not been copyrighted, and is not in the hands of any literary agent. The Gremlin characters are not creatures of his imagination as they are "well known" by the entire RAF and as far as I can determine no individual can claim credit.
>
> Therefore, I doubt that the name "Gremlin" can be copyrighted.

Feitel added that the payment for the story would be shared by Dahl and the RAF, but that Dahl probably "would accept any reasonable deal on our usual basis."

Two days later, on July 18, Kay Kamen wrote to Feitel:

Walt phoned and instructed me to see Dahl, obtain a copy of man-uscript *Gremlins* and forward copy to you for conference with Roy.

Despite this fevered interest, it still took awhile to formalize the deal. Kamen's note to Feitel dated August 3, 1942, states:

> As per copy of letter to Roy which I sent to you, you will understand the present situation. Apparently Dahl's contacts with Walt through Mrs. Mercier-Fairre [a Washington socialite that Dahl flirted with and who knew Walt casually] are interpreted by him as a proposition— one more liberal than my understanding of Walt's and Roy's wishes.

However, an arrangement was made with Dahl, and the Disney studio started devising ways to acquaint the American public with gremlins, develop a workable story with appropriate character designs, and estab-lish a copyright for Disney's version of gremlins just as it had for Disney's versions of the foreign folk tales of Snow White and Pinocchio.

In an essay by Dahl entitled *Lucky Break* (1978), the writer remembered his first two-week excursion to the Disney studio in November 1942:

> Because of the Gremlins, I was given three weeks' leave from my duties at the Embassy in Washington and whisked out to Hollywood. There, I was put up at Disney's expense in a luxurious Beverly Hills hotel and given a huge shiny car to drive about in.
>
> Each day, I worked with the great Disney at his studios in Burbank, roughing out the story-line for the forthcoming film. I had a ball. I was still only twenty-six. I attended story conferences in Disney's enormous office where every word spoken, every suggestion made, was taken down by a stenographer and typed out afterwards.
>
> I mooched around the rooms where the gifted and obstreperous animators worked, the men who had already created *Snow White, Dumbo, Bambi* and other marvelous films, and in those days, so long as these crazy artists did their work, Disney didn't care when they turned up at the studio or how they behaved. When my time was up, I went back to Washington and left them to it.

Dahl apparently made quite an impression when he was at the studio. By all accounts he played the role of the dashing, enthusiastic war hero and was very personable.

Walt threw a party in Dahl's honor on his first night in Hollywood. Among those attending were actors Spencer Tracy (Walt's polo buddy), William Powell, Dorothy Lamour, Greer Garson, and even Charlie Chaplin. One of the party games was having these distinguished screen stars act out different gremlins with Charlie Chaplin taking the prize for his inter-pretation of a widget.

Dahl even hooked up with the first of many of his Hollywood affairs, an actress and socialite named Phyllis Brooks nicknamed "Brooksie," who he treated so badly that she reportedly wanted to kill him just a few months after he had first succeeded in taking her to bed.

Walt was fond of nicknames and since Dahl was six-foot six-inches tall, Walt dubbed him "Stalky." Walt also had trouble pronouncing the name "Roald" correctly, so this helped him alleviate that situation.

Both Dahl and Walt had a fondness for the work of author Rudyard Kipling and the nickname supposedly came from a character of that same name in Kipling's *Stalky & Co.* (1899). The Kipling character was a tall, good-looking, charismatic, and mischievous boy at a British boarding school who demonstrated "stalkiness," meaning he was wily, ingenious, clever, and cunning.

In the story, Stalky goes on to become a heroic British soldier. Many reviewers found the character to be a self-righteous bully who escaped punishment because of his good looks and use of language. One reviewer in 1942 called the book "an unpleasant book about unpleasant boys at an unpleasant school" and that was not the harshest thing said about it and its characters.

However, Dahl had no problem accepting the nickname, especially since it was meant as a compliment, and sometimes signed his correspondence to Walt using the name Stalky.

In later years, Dahl always spoke fondly of Walt and of his treatment at the Disney studio.

On October 21, 1942, the Disney studio opened a story charge number for the gremlins project (#1551) which meant that expenses generated by the film could now be billed to that account. This meant Walt was serious about developing the film and was spending money to do so.

Curiously, around the same time it was announced that Dahl's gremlins would merely be a sequence in the Disney feature *Victory Through Airpower* (1943) being made at the same time and not a feature on its own. Obviously, this was an error, since it was clear Walt was looking at the property as an opportunity to get back into making an animated full-length entertainment feature.

When Dahl flew out to the studio to consult on the film, a studio press release proclaimed:

> Dahl is an authority on these little fellows, who wear suction boots so they can ride the wings of planes doing 400 miles an hour, and will give Disney benefit of his knowledge of them gained from personal experience as well as that of scores of other RAF pilots.

In a 1984 interview with Disney historian Robin Allan, Dahl remembered his time at the studio:

I think it was around 1942 and I was straight out of the RAF when I wrote *The Gremlins*. I invented the name and people saw it and someone showed it to Disney. He paid me for it. I gave the money to the RAF Benevolent Fund and they let me go out. I went out and they put me up in the Beverly Hills Hotel in great luxury, and I saw a lot of Disney.

They started to make the film in a very big way and I used to see them all every day—the animators—but Disney is the only one who interests you. He never drew anything; he did in the early days.

They got the storyboards up and started to make it in a very sort of casual way. Really, there's not much more to tell. I suppose I met him...oh...a dozen times. He used to shine at storyboards. He used to have those story conferences. The main thing is that Walt's ideas were the best ones.

Dahl spent ten days in Hollywood in April 1943 and despite his requirements at the studio itself (author Donald Sturrock pointed out that Dahl would mimic Walt's own stringent schedule of showing up at seven-thirty every morning and staying until seven or eight o'clock at night), he found plenty of time to entertain himself.

One evening he spent with actress Ginger Rogers and later went to Dorothy Lamour's wedding reception where he caught the eye of actress Marlene Dietrich.

To Walt's displeasure when he later found out, Dahl got so bored one day at the studio that he dragged off some of the storymen and artists to musician Hoagy Carmichael's elegant home in the Hollywood Hills. Carmichael and Dahl developed a friendship and Dahl even stayed at Carmichael's home later.

Dahl continued to elaborate on gremlins as the Disney staff lounged around Carmichael's pool.

An interview Dahl gave to the *Los Angeles Times* during his visit was the first time it was revealed that Walt planned on making a live-action film in which "only the little fellows themselves will be animated."

A test reel that has never resurfaced was shot in November 1942. Those who remember seeing the reel recall that there was a "good reception" to it and that primarily it featured live-action footage of planes with animated gremlins running about on them.

Both Dahl and Roy O. Disney lobbied to have the entire film done in animation and eventually Walt relented on that aspect, but not until March 1943.

Dahl imagined his name connected with a film that had the elaborate artistry of the early Disney animated feature films, despite the fact that

Walt was working with a smaller staff and some of his top artists were in the armed forces and unavailable.

In Roy's case, he felt it might save money on the costs of combining live action and animation since he had seen previous efforts were time-consuming and required intricate calculations that caused additional expenses.

The Disney studio had earlier combined live action and animation in MGM's *Hollywood Party* (1934) where Mickey Mouse interacts with comedian Jimmy Durante and in Fox Film Corporation's *Servant's Entrance* (1934) where actress Janet Gaynor has a nightmare where she is confronted by damaged kitchen utensils putting her on trial. Both were filmed in black and white.

The studio would later do successful and critically lauded short Technicolor segments combining live action and animation in the feature films *The Three Caballeros* (1944) and *Song of the South* (1946).

The idea of using live action (which would eliminate the problem of trying to animate realistic human characters) probably came from British-born writer Eric Knight who was briefly at the studio during this time period. He is perhaps best remembered for writing *Lassie Come Home* (1940). He also wrote clever, charming fantasy, such as the stories in his book *The Flying Yorkshireman* (1938).

Knight was hailed as comparable to America's James Thurber or Thorne Smith. *The Flying Yorkshireman* was ten stories about Sam Small, a villager in Yorkshire who has an endless repertoire of tall tales including one where he literally flies and gets into all sorts of mischief.

A tribute to the mustachioed Knight appears in 1943 Disney versions of the gremlin story in the form of a comedic RAF character called "Yorky."

In 1942, Knight went to work for Frank Capra's film unit which was producing the *Why We Fight* series. Disney had supplied some animation, primarily illustrated diagrams, for the series.

By July 1942, Knight was assigned to the Disney studio to assist in helping work out the details for the animation inserts of maps and diagrams which were featured in these documentaries.

Knight's letters to his wife from this time period reveal that Walt was actively wooing him to get involved in the gremlins project. The earliest reference appears in a letter dated August 17, 1942:

> This noon I talked with Walt. He is receptive, and we kid. He wants me to give him opinions on a swell idea—about Gremlins and Fifinellas and Widgets.

> Gremlins ride on R.A.F. planes with suction cup boots and drill bullet holes in planes. Fifinellas are girl Gremlins—all cousins to

a leprechaun. Widgets are young Gremlins born in a nest. I suggest he shoots the whole thing as a mixture of real R.A.F. and cartoon. So we laugh at lunch and I can kid him any way I want....

It was Knight's contention that if Walt wanted to create a sense of believability for the audience, the pilots and their planes should be shot in live action so that it seemed real. Then, the element of fantasy could be introduced by having the "imaginary" creatures done in animation and leverage the skills of Disney animators in drawing appealing little characters.

In a letter dated August 20, Knight wrote:

Walt thinks I'm aces—and is always kidding and asking me to work on the film [*The Gremlins*] RIGHT NOW. It's the only place I'd ever work in peacetime, because Walt's mind is light, funny and quick....

By September 4, 1942, Walt had become more serious about involving Knight as the latter was finishing his stint at the Disney studio. Knight wrote:

I'm at Disney's, and all cleared up with the odd papers collected and destroyed or returned to proper places. Well, so another Hollywood voyage is over...I had lots of "offers"—Walt wanted me to do the Gremlin story for cartoon films.

Knight died in a plane crash in January 1943 while on his way to Cairo to set up a new plan for Allied radio programming. Walt wrote to Knight's widow:

All of us here who worked with Eric had a tremendous respect and admiration for him.

Unfortunately, it was also a great loss to the gremlin project because Knight might have been the writer who could have helped focus the project since he had an impressive record of making British topics accessible and entertaining to American audiences.

No evidence exists of Dahl knowing of Knight's involvement and if he ever did, he never mentioned it.

By May 14, 1943, Walt had made his decision on who he wanted on the feature. Since Walt was still paying high weekly salaries to his staff who were not working on a feature film that could generate needed revenue, he loaded up all his top men on the project, especially since he saw that they were becoming as frustrated working on the government films as he was.

Dave Hand would be the overall director, a role he had filled on previous animated features like *Snow White* and *Bambi*. The directing animators would be Jack Kinney, Bill Roberts, Clyde Geronimi, Wilfred Jackson, and Ham Luske who would supervise the individual sequences in the film. This process had been established in the earlier feature films with great success.

Walt assigned Jim Bodrero who, along with Ted Sears, would be the primary shapers of the story, assisted by storymen T. Hee, Harry Reeves, Rex Cox, Ralph Wright, Bill Peet, and Elmer Plummer, as well as Marc Davis and Bill Justice who would also do animation.

The animation staff would include such recognized talents as Les Clark, Ward Kimball, Fred Moore, Ollie Johnston, Milt Kahl, John McManus, Eric Larson, and Norm Tate who were all still working at the studio and had not yet joined the armed forces for various reasons. Other top talents like Frank Thomas and Art Babbitt were in the service and so were unavailable.

Several possible scenarios were developed including the following two by storyman Ted Sears.

- The first scenario (November 1942) follows closely Dahl's story but adds a female love interest (a Women's Auxiliary Air Force officer) and an American fighter squadron who are an eager but incredulous audience for stories of gremlins. In the finale, the gremlins cooperated in turning the tide of battle during an enemy attack on the airfield.

- The second scenario (December 1942) had input from Dahl and made the female love interest a ferry pilot named Joan with a kid brother who had just joined the RAF. Gremlin Gus was given a Cockney accent to make him more lovable. A greater variety of gremlins were shown through a sequence where pilots were debriefed about their misadventures with the pixies of the air.

As usual, Walt had many artists submit possible art concepts for the gremlins.

Animator and story artist Retta Scott thought the project was so insignificant that she didn't list it (nor her work on the film *Victory Through Airpower*) in her autobiographical notes. She drew a comical-looking young boy in an ill-fitting flight suit. His pilot helmet had two green horns sticking out at the top, his black boats had multiple little suction cups on the bottom, and he had a pair of fairy-like wings on his back.

Even though Walt had others coming up with possible character designs as well, it is obvious that the final design that was used and is so familiar today was created by Bill Justice.

In an interview with author Rich Shale on January 29, 1976, animator Ward Kimball said:

> They tried to get that [*The Gremlins*] off the ground, but they just couldn't do it. It was cuter to talk about gremlins and things that happen, and nobody could decide on what a gremlin looked like. Walt never could decide in his mind what a gremlin should look like. It was as simple as that. Is it a little brownie?

Of course, a gremlin today would be easy to design in our open-ended imaginative way of going about things, but in those days, with everything so confined to a certain technique and Disney style, it was impossible. I think Walt got frustrated and gave it up. I remember that.

Between July 1942 and April 1943, despite the studio's ever-increasing deficit, Walt would invest at least $50,000 to develop Dahl's gremlins into a film. Little did either Dahl or Disney suspect that much like the notorious antics of the gremlins themselves, the project would be plagued by misfortune and make it seem like a cursed film.

CHAPTER SEVEN

Bill Justice Interview

Born in Dayton, Ohio, on February 9, 1914, Bill Justice grew up in Indianapolis, Indiana. He attended the John Herron Art Institute where he studied to be a portrait artist.

He joined the Disney studio in 1937 where he quickly rose from inbetweening to full animation. Justice served as an animator on animated features like *Bambi*, *Fantasia*, *Saludos Amigos*, *Victory Through Air Power*, *The Three Caballeros*, *Make Mine Music*, *Alice in Wonderland*, and *Peter Pan*.

The characters most closely associated with him are the chipmunks Chip'n'Dale, as he animated most of their appearances in the theatrical shorts.

During the 1950s, Justice directed several experimental shorts, including *Noah's Ark*, *A Symposium on Popular Songs*, and *The Truth About Mother Goose*, all of which were nominated for Academy Awards.

Along with Xavier ("X") Atencio, he also used the painstaking technique of stop-motion animation in live-action Disney features including *Babes in Toyland* and *Mary Poppins* as well as the opening titles for several live-action comedy features. In all, he contributed to fifty-seven animated shorts and nineteen features.

In 1955, Justice directed the animation of the "Mickey Mouse March" seen as the opening title segment of the original *Mickey Mouse Club* television show.

Walt Disney moved Justice to Walt Disney Imagineering (then known as WED) in 1965, where he programmed Audio-Animatronics figures for such Disneyland attractions as Great Moments with Mr. Lincoln, Mission to Mars, Pirates of the Caribbean, the Haunted Mansion, Country Bear Jamboree, and America Sings.

Justice went on to program the Hall of Presidents attraction at Walt Disney World. He also masterminded the creation of the Mickey Mouse Revue attraction featured at Walt Disney World and later, Tokyo Disneyland.

He was often called upon by the Disney company for special projects, from the design of the floats and costumes for the 1961 Disneyland

Christmas Parade to the artwork explaining the animation process using Disney characters in the August 1963 issue of *National Geographic* and a magnificent mural of Disney characters outside of the Walt Disney Story theater in the Magic Kingdom.

After forty-two years with the company, Justice retired in February 1979. He wrote a book in 1992 about his career at Disney called *Justice for Disney*. He received the Winsor McCay Award for Lifetime Achievement at the 2001 Annie Awards in Hollywood, and was inducted as a "Disney Legend" in 1996.

Even after his retirement, Justice was a popular Disney speaker at Disneyana conventions and at other venues, including voyages on the Norwegian Cruise Line and Donald Duck's 50th birthday celebrations.

The following is an excerpt from a much longer interview I did with Bill Justice in March 1997 when I was working as an animation instructor at the Disney Institute in Orlando, Florida. Two years later, at the second Disney Institute Animation Event in summer 1999, I asked some follow up questions.

JIM KORKIS: Bill, I'd like to talk about *The Gremlins* film project you were involved with during World War II.

BILL JUSTICE: That was quite awhile ago and my memory isn't as strong as it once was, but I'll try my best. I appreciate you showing me these pictures because that certainly helps. I loved those characters and I consider it one of the first big projects that Walt gave me, so I wanted to do my best.

JK: How did you end up being hired at Disney?

BJ: One day I saw an ad in *Esquire* magazine [June 1937] for jobs at Disney and everyone told me I was foolish and wouldn't hear back from them if I answered the ad. I answered that ad and they asked me to come to a tryout class at Disney.

Thirty days and there were thirty of us from all over the country. I was making $65.00 a week working two jobs and doing some freelance art and Disney offered me $12.00 a week and no guarantee of a job, but I was excited about working at Disney.

July 17, 1937, was my first day at Disney. I showed up wearing my best suit and that was a mistake. I wanted to make a good impression. Los Angeles was very, very hot and there was no air conditioning at the Hyperion studio, so the other guys looked at me like I was a hick. The next day I dressed more comfortably.

JK: Fairly early in your career, you worked on some of the classic animated features like *Bambi* (1942).

BJ: I did some animation of Bambi and Thumper on the ice. I loved that scene. I also did a scene where Bambi and his mother are discovering snow. Here is something for historians: I animated on the scene where Bambi's mother was running and she jumps a log and is shot and collapses in the snow. I animated on that and it was cut from the film. I didn't miss it. I preferred doing the stuff of Bambi and Thumper on ice.

JK: What were you doing at the Disney studio during World War II?

BJ: During the war, I worked on doing animation on shorts like *Der Fuerher's Face*, *Reason and Emotion*, and *The New Spirit*. I also did work on dozens of those training films the studio made which was the most boring thing in the world for an animator who had just finished drawing Bambi. It was all so technical and dry and you had to be very precise.

Hank Porter got swamped on doing insignias for the military, so I did maybe thirty or so of those. Hank did hundreds or thousands. I could draw just about every Disney character, so I was asked to help whenever I could. I liked doing it and wish I could have done more.

I was in good shape and expected to be drafted at any minute but never did. I think Walt had something to do with some of us staying at the studio rather than going into the service, but nobody ever told me. I had volunteered as a combat artist and thought I had the training to be valuable, but they never took me.

I visited military hospitals and did charcoal portraits of the service men there. They seemed to like that. There were eight of us who were part of that group and doing that work taught me a lot.

Portraits just always interested me because one of the hardest things an artist can do is make a portrait that looks like you. It was quite a challenge. We always felt you can't tell if a tree looks like the tree or not, but you can sure tell if a portrait looks like you.

I studied to be a portrait artist, but it was a lousy way to make a living. I was fortunate enough to do a few of them before I went to Disney. It is a great satisfaction doing a portrait.

We did some "camp shows" for some military installations in southern California to entertain the troops. Ward Kimball had a band, not the later Firehouse Five but something like the Huggajeedy 8, that played, and we also performed this real corny melodrama called *Curse You, Jack Dalton!* that always got laughs.

I did an act where I was billed as "The World's Fastest Sketch Artist" and drew ten or fifteen sketches of Disney characters while Kimball's band played two or three numbers.

I was always a fast artist. The big finale was this live girl dancing on stage and I was drawing her life size on this six-foot-tall easel and pretending to measure her various body parts as I was drawing. Another girl would run in and pin a pair of panties on my drawing in the appropriate area. It was a lot of fun and very corny, but the audience loved it.

I also did sketches of their favorite Disney characters for the men.

JK: At this time, you became involved with the Roald Dahl gremlins project.

BJ: When RAF Flight Lieutenant Roald Dahl came to the studio to work on his gremlins project, I was assigned to draw these little creatures according to his description. They were like six inches high and made a lot of mischief at the Royal Air Force.

There were female gremlins called fifinellas and children of gremlins called widgets and higher altitude gremlins called spandules. As I recall, the project for me began as a book, not a movie.

Dahl dictated the story and I made pencil illustrations for his approval. I was influenced by the work Fred Moore had done on the dwarfs for *Snow White*. He could put such appeal into his drawings of small people. He was short himself. I have some of his drawings and am still in awe of how he was able to do it.

Having worked on Thumper in *Bambi* and the "Pastoral Symphony" segment of *Fantasia*, I had gotten the reputation of being able to do cute characters.

The gremlins had to be cute so you would have sympathy for them even when they were doing these terrible things like destroying these planes fighting the Nazis.

I know Walt had a lot of other artists working on the gremlin characters as well. I don't recall seeing any of it, but I probably did. Nothing sticks in my mind. Walt always used to have others working on something so he could get plenty of options and pick the best one.

JK: What was Dahl like?

BJ: Dahl was a ruggedly handsome man and a war hero. He had been shot down in Africa while strafing German troops and planes. I guess he had been injured pretty badly, but it wasn't obvious when you looked at him. He did have a slight limp, but it never slowed him down.

All the girls were crazy for him. I felt invisible when I accompanied him to parties. He loved all that attention from women. And that accent! He just exuded confidence and that he knew what he was doing even if he didn't.

Once he offered to drive me to a meeting and promptly started down the left side of the street. That's how they did it in England, you know. From then on, I drove.

He was very charming and I think Walt really liked him and liked having him around. At that time, Walt was very interested in aviation.

JK: Why did Walt cancel the film?

BJ: Work just dragged on and on. Everyone thought it would be easy to come together, but it wasn't for some reason. Walt figured by the time the picture would've been completed the war was going to be over and so what's the point? People wouldn't be interested anymore. So they stopped work on it.

That sometimes happened at the studio that you could put in years on a project and then it got shelved and you never knew why. Walt knew if something just wasn't working and no matter how much time and money he had put into it, he would put it away until he felt it was ready. I don't think Walt really liked war stories or religious stories and that might have been one of the reasons.

The project wasn't a total loss. This was the first time I'd been asked to create a new cartoon character rather than working from somebody else's model sheet. That was very exciting. My version pretty much became the model sheet.

A good artist named Al Dempster added some full-page color paintings to my penciled illustrations and the book *The Gremlins* was published by Random House. It was the first book I'd ever illustrated and it was quite a thrill, let me tell you. It was an expanded version of Dahl's story that I illustrated for *Cosmopolitan* magazine.

In my copy of the book, there is a written "thank you" note from Walt on a front page with my drawing of a gremlin looking down an open manhole. It says, "To Bill Justice—With Thanks and Appreciation for a Swell Job. Sincerely, Walt Disney."

It means a lot to me. If you knew Walt, that was his way of saying that it wasn't my fault that the project got cancelled, that he knew I had tried my best.

JK: Do you ever still think about those characters and that project?

BJ: In 1970 I was out in Orlando, Florida, programming audio-animatronics for Walt Disney World that was due to open soon. I was using one of those old consoles that had the black dials on it. It was certainly an improvement over our original method that included scoring cuts in a stack of discs, but it was still time consuming.

People forget that audio-animatronics characters are just heavy machines. That's what they are, not real people. Programming with those early crude systems is difficult to describe and difficult to accomplish.

You'd program one part and then have to set it and then rewind to program another part happening at the same time and so on. There was a lot of waiting time involved getting anything done.

Out of boredom, on the console I would do these small pencil sketches of Disney characters like Donald Duck and Chip'n'Dale to amuse myself and those I worked with.

One time I sketched two gremlins on their knees playing dice in about the middle and a larger sketch of a gremlin at the top of the console looking down on the other sketches. I had to explain to people that they were Disney characters just like Mickey Mouse and Goofy. They had never heard or seen them before.

I just thought it was fitting to have gremlins messing with the audio-animatronics. Years later I was surprised but pleased that the console still exists on display in DACS (Digital Animation Control System) in the utilidors under the Magic Kingdom, even though that type of console is no longer used. Things are always getting more sophisticated. I guess somebody got a kick out of those drawings and felt they should keep them around rather than erasing or tossing them.

JK: Any finals thoughts on the gremlins?

BJ: I just loved them and loved working on them. I am sorry the film never got made, but we just couldn't whip the story together. That happens sometimes and you move on to something else.

JK: Thanks for sharing these memories.

BJ: My pleasure. When you get older, the first thing that goes is your legs, then your eyesight, then your love life, then your memory, then your... (long pause)...oh, I forget (laughs).

CHAPTER EIGHT

The "Cosmopolitan" Story and Clause 12

One of Walt's plans to popularize the proposed film and to acquaint Americans with gremlins was to have a short story about them appear in the December issue of *Cosmopolitan* magazine illustrated by the Disney studio.

Dahl, without using an agent as an intermediary, contacted the U.S. general interest magazines *American Magazine, Liberty*, and *Collier's* about publishing his story. He leveraged the story's connection with Disney as a way to get them interested in it, but was overly self-assured about the merits of his own writing even though he had only one short story published and that one may have been heavily edited by writer C.S. Forester.

Collier's proposed cutting the story in half. *American Magazine* indicated it would be willing to run two pages of full-color Disney art on the project, but felt that the "fiction flopped." The editor said they might be interested if a more experienced writer worked with Dahl on the story, but hesitated to suggest it because of Dahl's cockiness about his own ability.

Collier's did publish an article featuring gremlins entitled "What Every Pilot Knows" by Quentin Reynolds for its October 31, 1942, issue with full-color watercolor artwork by former Disney artist Gustaf Tenggren.

"It's no joke to be sitting up at 20,000 feet and hear them chattering among themselves out on the wings," stated one caption underneath the painting of nine little men with huge puffy hats doing damage to a Spitfire in flight.

Finally, Dahl was forced to work with Harold Matson, the agent of C.S. Forester, Dahl's friend who had helped him get his first story printed in a magazine. Matson was able to make a deal with *Cosmopolitan*.

In a letter to Walt Disney dated September 4, 1942, *Cosmopolitan* editor Frances Whiting wrote:

> It gives me the greatest pleasure to tell you that *Cosmopolitan* has already sent the necessary printed pamphlet of *The Gremlins* to the

Bureau of Copyrights in Washington, D.C., and that our rights and yours are protected.

I am sure Lt. Dahl told you that *Cosmopolitan* would be happy to assign the copyright to you at the proper time. We are delighted beyond words to have this story and to know that your magic touch will bring it to the screen.

Lt. Dahl tells me that you are a pilot. Therefore, I suppose that at this very moment a Gremlin is sitting on your shoulder reading my words. Truly, I think I must learn to fly. Sincerely, FW.

Walt assigned animator Bill Justice, who had demonstrated an ability to draw cute characters, to work with Dahl and do illustrations for the project.

In a letter dated September 1, 1942, Dahl not only gave some suggestions on illustrating this story, but casually states that his chief, Air Commodore H.N. Thornton, would be visiting the studio to discuss the RAF's involvement in the project. The Air Ministry was insisting on "the R.A.F. having the power to say 'no' to anything that is done."

Walt was unhappy with this turn of events, but his interest in the film, his recent experience in dealing with the military and its rules and processes, as well as the fact that profits from all merchandise and promotions would go to the RAF Benevolent Fund could only help legitimize the project.

However, the desire of the Air Ministry for final approval, which was egged on by Dahl himself citing possible embarrassment to the RAF, resulted in a provision known as Clause 12 of the contract.

The infamous clause quoted in a memo from Roy Disney to Walt on October 23, 1942, guaranteed among other things that Disney was obligated to keep Dahl informed of the development of the gremlin project "to the end that the said air attache [Dahl] may furnish such advice and suggestions as may enable the British Air Ministry to approve the final version of said motion picture."

As Richard Shale points out in his outstanding thesis, *Donald Duck Joins Up* (1976), the implication of the wording is "that final control over content rested not with the Disney studio but with the British Air Ministry".

In a letter to his mother dated November 10, 1942, Dahl wrote about this "marvelous clause":

> [It gives me] full power to disapprove of any part of the film at any stage of its production. I don't know how many million dollars [Walt might spend] on making the film and [if] I still don't like it, I can just say "Stuff it up" and he has to.

The contract was sent to Dahl on September 23, 1942, with a letter from Frank Waldheim explaining:

Pursuant to our recent telephone conversation, I enclose three copies of the proposed agreement regarding the Gremlins with certain portions redrafted in conformity with our discussion…. If there are any questions, Mr. Roy Disney and I will be glad to confer with you regarding the contract.

I hope that you will understand that Mr. Disney has every desire to exclude from the motion picture anything which would be in bad taste. This desire is prompted both by his own natural inclination and by the knowledge that it would be commercially unsound to produce a picture offensive to either American or British sensibilities.

However, it is important that the Air Attache's approval should be exercised before the picture goes into production—because, in the day-by-day "shooting" of the picture, there would not be time for consulting the Air Attache regarding the details of the various scenes. I hope that the proposed clauses properly express the thoughts of the Air Attache in the matter.

However, Dahl delayed signing and explained why in a letter to Walt dated October 7, 1942:

Your brother Roy came down here the other day and we had some very pleasant conversations. As is only natural, I have got a lawyer to check over your contract and he said that there were one or two things which he would like to discuss with Franklin Waldheim in New York before I signed it.

Roy was a little disappointed and, quite frankly, so was I, because I have not got a great deal of time for lawyers and their like. On the other hand, having placed the matter in his hands, I am letting him go through with it. I think everything should be cleared up in the very near future.

Finally, Roy Disney wrote to Walt on October 26, 1942, and included a discussion of the infamous Clause 12:

We now have in the studio the fully executed contract with Lt. Dahl on the Gremlin story. The contract provides that the copyright on the first magazine story in *Cosmopolitan* and any subsequent ones will be assigned to us.

Cosmopolitan had advised Frank Waldheim that they will assign to us just as soon as published. It is to come out in the December issue and will appear about November first, which is sometime next week.

So, with this article and its accompanying illustrations, our copyright will be effective very soon. It will be an international copyright through publication in Canada simultaneously.

Regarding the R.A.F. approval, this paragraph in the contract is the way the matter was finally worked out: Clause 12.

"The purchaser will keep the Air Attache of the British Embassy advised from time to time of the development of the story treatment of the motion picture to be based upon said work, to the end that the said Air Attache may furnish such advice and suggestions as may enable the British Air Ministry to approve the final version of said motion picture.

"The British Embassy or the Air Attache thereof, shall have the right, at no cost or expense to the purchaser, to designate a technical advisor to make his headquarters at the studio of the purchaser, for the purpose of consulting and advising with the purchaser in connection with the production of any picture hereunder."

Walt had some legitimate production concerns about this stipulation which are reflected in a letter he wrote to Dahl on October 1, 1942:

I talked to Commander Thornton regarding approval of our shooting script and I see no reason why this cannot be handled without any trouble. We would want this film to be satisfactory to the R.A.F. in every way.

Our only concern is that we do not want someone to find petty faults or assume a picayunish attitude after the film is completed and thereby put us to considerable expense in making changes. Therefore, if someone could be assigned to check our work while it is in production, it would be much more satisfactory to everyone concerned.

Walt called the art editor of *Cosmopolitan* to plead for extra time to develop illustrations for Dahl's story. *Cosmopolitan* responded they wanted the sketches by September 15 at the latest, which prompted Walt's to reply, "We couldn't possibly set the character in so short a time."

Walt pointed out that everyone seemed to have his own idea of what gremlins looked like. He mentioned a recent newspaper article reporting gremlins "riding on our Flying Fortresses—in other words, there is an American branch of gremlins."

Dahl did not help matters at all. In the *Washington Daily News*, Dahl told an interviewer that "Disney has tried twelve times to draw the right picture and hasn't gotten it yet. But it will come."

Later, Dahl shared with Virginia Wright in a *Los Angeles Times* interview:

He [Dahl] comes onto the Disney lot with very definite ideas about the appearance of Gremlins. Their make-up is not to be left to the imagination of Disney artists.

The December 1942 issue of *Cosmopolitan* featured Senator Harry S. Truman's piece on "Let's Quit Stalling and Get Tough!" and actress Ann Sothern's article on "How to Get Along With Women."

However, the entire editorial page for that issue spotlighted a piece that the magazine proclaimed was "unquestionably the greatest contribution to living folklore in more than a hundred years. It is destined to live long after this war has been forgotten". That unforgettable seven page story was "Introducing the Gremlins" by "Pegasus" and illustrated by the Disney studio.

Pegasus was the winged flying horse of mythology and the pseudonym was apparently necessary because Dahl had not yet received the official sanction of both Lord Halifax, the British ambassador in Washington, D.C., and the RAF to be identified as the author.

His short story "Shot Down Over Libya" similarly did not identify Dahl specifically, but was credited to an anonymous RAF pilot. This restriction on identification was to maintain military secrecy about pilots and their squadrons because the information might be used by the enemy.

There were also restrictions on serving officers to be identified on some written work because it would be assumed that they personally represented the RAF's views. The sanction was granted by the time of the release of the book six months later where Dahl is fully credited as the author.

The editorial even reflected Dahl's distinctive humor when the author of the gremlin story pointed out that the money would go to the RAF Emergency Fund, but "there is provision in the contract for enough money to buy me a new tooth."

Later, Dahl would use the royalties from his short story "Shot Down Over Libya" to buy an elaborate new set of false teeth, crafted by Lord Halifax's dentist with a plate made of gold and platinum costing $350. The eccentric Dahl had had his healthy teeth removed long before his famous crash in order to avoid a future of infections, toothaches, and expensive dental treatments.

The editorial continued:

> Pegasus does not claim to be the creator of the Gremlins. Nobody really knows, he says, how the legend started. There are many versions of the origin of these wonderful little creatures. What Pegasus did, with the approval of the British authorities, was to set down the most widely accepted version of their origin and exploits.
>
> As with any living legend, word-of-mouth accounts vary, and it's the writer's job to select and embellish the best stand to raise the whole story to the level of literature. How splendidly Pegasus has fulfilled this task you'll discover in this issue of *Cosmopolitan, where for the first time the complete approved version of the Gremlins appears.*

The editorial could not control its enthusiasm for what it described was "the greatest legend born in our time" from the "real man behind the pen name, handsome in the uniform of the RAF, well over six-feet tall and with just the eyes and smile he should have had."

It went on:

> Peagus was careful to warn us that several of the Gremlins were now in our office. Not being fliers, we couldn't see them, of course. They are jealous little people and will be watching every move you make on their story, he reminded us. If you leave any of them out, beware.

> So far, there have been no suspicious occurrences and our Art Director who flew out to work with Walt Disney's staff on the drawings, assures us that there was no Gremlin trouble in Hollywood.

While the illustrations are credited to the Disney studio, they were the work of a young animator named Bill Justice, with Mary Blair supplying the full color paintings.

A note from Hal Adelquist to Walt dated June 3, 1943, reveals that Bill Justice even contributed some story ideas:

> I was talking to Bill Justice yesterday regarding the Gremlin script and thought that perhaps you might be interested in a slant that we thought appropriate. Bill, as you know, has designed some little woodland Gremlins which look like exciting characters and the thought occurred to us that we might start our story with the Gremlins in the woods.

> They are a colorful little group and we show them in their various moods, work and play. Perhaps these little people could be a very democratic group and Gremlin Gus is the elected President of the Gremlins. One day a terrific earthquake occurs which actually is caused by the Caterpillar tractors and bulldozers tearing up the wooded section.

> It is a national calamity as far as the Gremlins are concerned and Gremlin Gus summons the Gremlins to the top of a hill overlooking the new field whereupon he issues a declaration of war against the intruders. We would then treat the story through the eyes of the Gremlins as they attack the Spitfires instead of through the eyes of the pilots, etc.

Animator Mark Kausler was the first person to confirm that the paintings in the *Cosmopolitan* version (as opposed to the book version) were the work of Mary Blair, who is perhaps best remembered today for her design work on many Disney animated features, including *Saludos Amigos* and *Alice in Wonderland*, as well as her distinctive work for the Disney theme park attraction, "it's a small world."

In Dahl's letter to his mother dated November 27, 1942, he shared an incident where Walt exploded over a piece of color artwork Blair had drawn for the story that he didn't like. Dahl quoted Walt as saying:

> Goddamit, Mary, I have to buy the stories, direct the pictures, produce them, but son of a bitch, I'm buggered if I'm going to draw the illustrations as well.

Significantly, the *Cosmopolitan* editorial ended with:

> The Gremlins is the greatest contribution to living folklore in more than a hundred years. It is destined to live long after this war has been forgotten.
>
> The Gremlins belong with the immortals of literature because they express the invincible human spirit creating out of war and brutality the antidote for these very things; they demonstrate the miraculous human mind at work translating unendurable strain into gaiety and beauty.
>
> Just so, we believe, will that same human spirit build beauty and peace again into this tired world.

There are some interesting differences between the seven-page story in *Cosmopolitan* and the forty-eight page version that would later be published in book form by Random House in the United States.

Some of these changes are fairly minor, such as "Americanizing" British expressions or shortening or dropping a sentence or two in the book version. Other changes are more extensive, including deletions and additions of material.

Whether these changes are examples of Dahl's growth as a storyteller to go back and edit his original draft or whether they represent the input of Walt's story crew during the months between the magazine and book publication is a matter of conjecture, but overall, they made the slender material a stronger story. However, the basic story remained the same.

For the interest of brevity, the following summary lists just some of the changes between the two versions.

The *Cosmopolitan* story begins with the legend of the gremlin clan that lived happily in a beautiful green wood until 1940 when humans arrived in lorries and tore down the wood, paved it over, and built an airplane factory. It was then the gremlins swore they would accompany those who flew the planes and "harry him and tease him and worry him until they obtained some sort of satisfaction for all the harm they had done."

Dahl described the imps as having "funny horns growing out of their heads and funny clothes which they made out of leaves sewed together with long shoots of grass." The illustrations did not resemble this description; instead, the gremlins were in sort of aviation flight suits.

In the book, Dahl moves this opening legend to later in the story after both the pilot Gus and Gremlin Gus are introduced to the readers. He has pilot Gus recount the story and now instead of wearing woodland garb, the gremlins conform to the Disney illustrations and wear "funny boots on their funny feet, and with these boots—and this was the funniest of all—they could walk upside down under the branches of trees."

In the *Cosmopolitan* story, Dahl's gremlins had suction-cup boots to stay on airplanes, but in the book he wisely decided to introduce the concept earlier and come up with a logical reason for this ancient tribe to wear such footwear.

In the book, men in "lorries" became men in "great trucks" as all the British terms like "getting on the blower" for using the telephone became Americanized in the book version to appeal to a larger audience.

In the book, Dahl now has the gremlins describe the airplanes as "tin birds" and the gremlins' goal was now expanded to "follow those big tin birds wherever they go to get revenge for the loss of our homes. We will make mischief for them, and we will harry and tease the men who fly them, until we obtain some satisfaction for all the harm that has been done to us".

After the recounting of the legend, the *Cosmopolitan* version of the story mirrors the opening of the book version almost word-for-word with only minor changes:

> It was some time during the Battle of Britain when Hurricanes and Spitfires were up from dawn to dusk and the noise of battle was heard all day in the sky; when the English countryside from Thanet to Severn was dotted with the wreckage of planes.

> It was in the early autumn, when the chestnuts were ripening and the apples were beginning to drop off the trees—it was then that the first gremlins were seen by the Royal Air Force.

A pilot named Gus (but obviously patterned very closely in physical appearance and attitude to Dahl himself) was patroling in his Hurricane fighter at 18,000 feet over Dover when he noticed on his wing a little man "scarcely more than six inches high, with a large round face and a little pair of horns growing out of his head. On his legs were a pair of shiny black suction boots which enabled him to remain standing on the wing at 300 miles an hour."

The little man had a hand drill almost as big as himself and was busily engaged in boring four holes in the wing. Despite flick rolls to dislodge the intruder, the little man clambered on to the engine and drilled a neat hole in it.

In the *Cosmopolitan* version, the gremlin puts on an asbestos suit before doing so—just one example of the many tangential details in the magazine version which were eventually eliminated from the final book version to aid the flow of the story.

The sabotage forces the flyer to do an emergency landing on the Dover-London road. When Gus' sergeant points out that the damage to the wing and engine cowling were bullets, Gus' reply is, "Those aren't bullet holes. A Gremlin did that."

The *Cosmopolitan* version gives the reply to Gus, but the book version oddly assigns credit for that historical moment to a fitter named Barry, possibly an aviation friend of Dahl's, who never again appears in the story.

Soon the word spread throughout the RAF "like a prairie fire." Gus recounts his tale with his squadron buddies in the mess at drinking time. However, one of his friends (nicknamed "Stuffy") refuses to believe in gremlins until an angry Gremlin Gus appears and shoves Stuffy's mug of beer smashing to the floor.

Gremlin Gus is described as having:

> [A] strawberry nose which looked like the moon through a telescope, and his head with its stubby horns, was as bald as could be. He was wearing a little red bridge jacket, with a pair of well-cut corduroy trousers to match and on his head, tilted at as much of an angle as his horns would allow, was a green derby. And of course he had on his shiny black suction boots.

Apparently, Dahl insisted on the derby/bowler hat and Gremlin Gus became the only gremlin who wears one, although it is obvious the Disney artists struggled unsuccessfully to include it as part of the design. It looks awkward and out of place on the flight helmet, despite each new illustration moving the hat to a different location on the head to try and make it work.

Three days later, another pilot nicknamed "Jamface" burst into the mess announcing he has seen a fifinella, a female gremlin. Again, Stuffy is ready to dismiss this new discovery until, with a rustle of silk, a fifinella scampered across the table with "her small, elegant, curly horns" and "handsome white buckskin boots buttoned all the way up front with a row of tiny buttons."

It was obvious that gremlins had come to stay since the base was now plagued by many incidents of gremlin mischief including Gus being distracted at night by a gremlin which results in a forced landing in a plowed field and the episode of the nautical-minded gremlin who wore a sailor suit with a little yellow Mae West life vest over it who drilled a hole in Jamface's gas tank looking for his boat.

Fortunately, the mischief was temporarily diverted when gremlin Jamface, who had taken a fancy to being fed used postage stamps by pilot Jamface, repaired the damage.

In the book version, Dahl includes an interlude where Gus and Gremlin Gus are shot down over the English Channel and during the four hours they floated awaiting rescue, Gus convinced the gremlin to join forces against the unnamed enemy—neither the words "Hitler" or "Nazi" appear in either version of the story, although the word "German" appears on occasion as an adjective.

Pilot Gus passionately pleaded:

> Look here—these tin birds are planes, and they're helping us fight to save our homes—and your home, too. If you help us win this fight, we'll give you gremlins the deepest wood in England for your very own.

A few days later, Pilot Jamface burst into the mess where his compatriots are drinking to announce he has found a nest of twelve widgets. In the *Cosmopolitan* version, a widget is a young male gremlin and a flippety-gibbet is a young fifinella. In the book, all widgets are the young of gremlins and fifinellas and in each nest of twelve, only one will eventually turn into a fifinella.

Again, Stuffy, who never seems to learn, declares the existence of widgets as nonsense. So naturally, the widgets appear and get a hold of Stuffy's lit cigarette and drive "the hot end like a battering ram into his ankle."

In the *Cosmopolitan* version, Dahl takes time to describe widgets in great detail which is absent from the book version:

> They all had little horns and little faces and the Widgets were all dressed in little red smocks and little green shorts, but unlike their fathers, the Gremlins, they had no suction boots; they merely wore little brown shoes with crepe rubber soles. And, of course, they didn't have derby hats.
>
> The Flipperty-Gibbets had on little short blue dresses instead of the crinolines that their mothers, the Fifinellas, wore: but they didn't have suction boots either. Just little white shoes with crepe rubber soles.

The description was apparently deleted in the book version since it didn't match the Disney design for widgets. But while the book version edits down the widget encounter, it includes an entirely new section not even hinted at in the *Cosmopolitan* version: Stuffy's discovery of spandules.

> [Spandules are] a breed of high altitude gremlins to be found only above thirty thousand feet. They live in the rolling valleys of huge, white cumulus clouds, and all day they eat hailstones. They're at least three times as big as ordinary gremlins and their bodies are specially designed for high altitude work.
>
> They're covered with long, black hair to protect them against the terrific cold, and their faces look rather like oxygen masks—which probably helps them to breathe the thin air. Their bodies are flat and thin, and therefore not affected by the pressure.

They also had no legs, just short arms with suction gloves on their hands and apparently melted away into a damp patch if they dropped below thirty thousand feet.

Both the *Cosmopolitan* version and the book version recount that ten days after the widget incident, Pilot Gus decides to go up in the air on a mission despite being sick with the flu and a temperature of 102 degrees. Of course, a whole group of untrained, mischievous gremlins also hop on board and disrupt everything. (In the *Cosmopolitan* version, it is because they are trying to catch up to a fifinella who had just seductively taken off on another Hurricane.)

When Gus is in the air, he spots a German plane and when he engages it in battle, the German rear gunner rakes the Hurricane from stem to stern and Gus ends up with a bullet through his kneecap and another in his ankle. As he tries to land his crippled plane, Gus sees thousands of gremlins pick up the entire landing field and run with it for a hundred yards and set it back down so that Gus crashes exactly 100 yards away from the runway.

Gus languished in the hospital for weeks and during that time comes up with the idea of setting up a gremlin training school in one of the hangars.

The gremlins had to undergo two separate courses of training. Initial Training School (ITS) was run by Gremlin Gus who gave the gremlins negative reinforcement when they tried to sabotage a practice plane. For instance, when they try to bore holes in the wings, they are squirted with old engine oil. If they jumped on the wings, they dropped into a bucket of green paint—or India ink in the *Cosmopolitan* version.

Also in the *Cosmomopolitan* version, if they fiddled with the bomb doors they were chased by a woffledigit who looks like a wolf with six legs. All gremlins "firmly believe that woffledigits feed on nothing but gremlins, but as a matter of fact they are quite harmless and won't touch anything but used motor oil".

Perhaps at the urging of Disney storymen, Dahl wisely drops woffledigits in the book version since it needlessly adds another new character to complicate the storyline. In their place, he substituted a nasty electrical shock as the negative reinforcement.

The Advanced Training School (ATS) was run by Gremlin Jamface. While the gremlins had been cured of being bad, they had not been taught to be good, and that was the purpose of ATS.

Gremlin Jamface went around with a satchel of used postage stamps and when the gremlins were confronted with a broken-down plane, they were rewarded with some of their favorite food if they straightened a propeller blade or stopped the leaks and de-iced the wings. He would pop a used stamp in his own mouth when he thought no one was looking and thus always had a bad case of indigestion.

The two courses were so successful that other RAF stations sent their gremlins for training.

Just after Christmas, Gus came out of the hospital to rejoin his squadron, but it was not the same as before, since he now walked with a slight limp (just like Dahl) and had failed to pass a required medical exam three times which he had to pass in order to fly again.

Gremlin Gus summoned a conference of gremlins and they decided to help Gus pass the medical exam. Hundreds of them crowded the examination room. "Naturally the medico didn't see them; only pilots and navigators and air gunners and people who fly can see those things."

The gremlins helped Gus pass the test where he had to jump up and down on a chair ten times and then have his pulse return to normal quickly. They pushed his leg forward when it was tapped by the doctor. Most importantly, all the gremlins, fifinellas, and widgets helped when Gus had to close his eyes and balance on his bad leg.

Remarkably, Gus passed the tests. There was much celebrating, with Gus singing songs and toasting his small benefactors with tankards of strong ale while the gremlins feasted on used postage stamps.

The *Cosmopolitan* version ends here. The book version takes another two paragraphs to remind the reader that with the help of gremlins, a pilot who learned to love them, fear them, and respect them was able to return to flying, but it is indeed an unhappy man who goes up into the sky to fight saying, "I do not believe in gremlins."

The story was popular enough for *Good Housekeeping* magazine in England to want to reprint it. Dahl sent Walt a letter dated January 2, 1943, which stated in part:

> *Cosmopolitan* have been on to me regarding an enquiry which they have had from *Good Housekeeping* magazine in England who want to publish the Gremlins story.
>
> Personally, I am rather against it because it would spoil the market a little for your book over there. The question of keeping the idea going does not arise at all in England because, as you know, there is no danger of it fading out there so long as the war is on. Provided you agree, therefore, I am going to ask *Cosmopolitan* to turn it down.

Roy Disney replied on January 6, 1943:

> For your information, Mr. Franklin Waldheim, our New York attorney, has already written us concerning the request of *Cosmopolitan* to permit the Gremlin story, as published in their December issue, to be republished in the *Good Housekeeping* magazine in England. We have told Mr. Waldheim that we would have no objection to this being done, but that it would be subject to your approval.

Dahl, of course, did not approve. He had become increasing possessive and protective of the property to the point of preventing opportunities that would have allowed it to develop along the normal Disney marketing process.

Interestingly, in a letter Dahl sent to Walt October 4, 1942, he enthused:

> I received a telegram the other day from a big publisher in England [Hamish Hamilton Limited] who wants to publish my story in full in a booklet form, but this is of course entirely your concern.

> I think we should put this out as soon as you have started on the film and standardized your characters, and I do think it would be unwise to wait too long with it, because the whole subject is gaining to such an extent now that I feel sure there will be other books and other artists competing in this field in the near future.

In fact, there had been numerous requests to expand the story and publish it as a book, and that idea appealed to Walt.

Of course, Dahl insisted that he did not care at all for illustrations in *Cosmopolitan* and wrote to Walt:

> Another point, of course, entails a completely new set of drawings from you, because the ones you originally gave *Cosmopolitan* would not be suitable.

For one thing, Dahl pointed out that none of the drawings showed the gremlins wearing derby hats. He wrote to Walt on September 22, 1942:

> *Cosmopolitan* have just sent me down three rather bad Photostat copies of the drawings which you were good enough to rush through for them.

> I am terribly glad to see that you have been able to make a start and have overcome the difficulties you had in deciding what a Gremlin was like. If I had been able to come down and talk with you about them, I know I could have, at any rate, given you an accurate description of what they looked like.

> I must say that you have got very close to the mark. I would like to mention, however, and I do hope that you won't mind my pointing this out, that the athletic Gremlin never wears a flying helmet, but always wears the regulation green bowler hat, because his duties never make it necessary for him to take the air.

> Don't you think he would look better in a bowler hat?

> I do wish you could let me see any other tentative drawings which you make of the little men, because I really do know what they look like, having seen a great number of them in my time, and I would be only too glad to give you any help I could.

Walt replied in a letter dated October 1, 1942:

> I have your letter of the 22nd regarding the *Cosmopolitan* Photostats. I think when you have seen the finished work you will like it much better. It is perhaps a little late to add the boller [sic] hats. However, there will be plenty of opportunity to bring them out later.

Dahl replied in a letter dated October 7, 1942:

> I am very glad to see that you had not very definite views about Gremlins not wearing bowler hats (which I think are called derbys in this country); but their omission in your drawings did cause a little trouble, because *Cosmopolitan* wanted to cut out my description of Gremlins because it did not tie up with your drawings.
>
> I am afraid that I took a very strong line with them and told them, just because you happened to have drawn a Gremlin slightly differently to what he really looks like, this does not mean that all the Gremlins in the world will suddenly change to conform with your drawings.
>
> After all, one may as well say that if you drew an elephant that looked rather like a horse, all elephants in every part of the world will henceforth look like horses, which is of course incorrect. I therefore told them that they had to leave my original description in, whether it tallied with your drawings or not. I hope you don't disapprove of this, but it is rather important to describe a thing as one sees it and as it exists.

Dahl was able to convince *Cosmopolitan* and Disney to allow the story and the illustrations to be reprinted in the *RAF Christmas Journal*.

With his usual playfulness and brashness, Dahl even ghost-wrote a joking introduction to the story apparently by Walt himself asking the aviation readers to capture a gremlin "and have him crated and shipped to California. I can assure you he'll be treated with the utmost care and consideration at this end."

The magazine appearance was perhaps too successful because it sparked an eager anticipation in the potential audience, but the actual production was not even close to getting started.

CHAPTER NINE

The Random House Book

The continuing development at the Disney studio in terms of story and character concept art is keenly reflected in the book publication that differed in some interesting ways from the story as it was published in *Cosmopolitan* magazine less than a year earlier.

The publication of *The Gremlins: From the Walt Disney Production A Royal Air Force Story by Flight Lieutenant Roald Dahl* in 1943 by Random House consisted of a 50,000 copy print run for the U.S. market.

The book was forty-eight pages in length, more of an extended short story than a novel, and sold out within the first six months. Because of the length and the use of cartoon fantasy characters, the book has often been categorized as a children's book, especially since it was from Disney.

The copyright page stated: "All rights reserved throughout the world by Walt Disney Productions." It also stated that it was "designed and produced by Artists & Writers Guild, Inc." as well as the fact that "The R.A.F. Benevolent Fund will receive the author's share of the proceeds from the sale of this book."

All the black-and-white illustrations were done by Bill Justice. The thirteen color illustrations in the story were by Al Dempster who was a background artist at the studio. At the time he was working on *Victory Through Air Power*, among other projects, and in the 1950s, he would illustrate many of the Little Golden Books featuring Disney characters.

Dahl ordered fifty copies of the book which he used to promote himself. He gave away copies to important acquaintances, such as the British ambassador in Washington, Lord Halifax, who sent a note of thanks, and the First Lady of the United States Eleanor Roosevelt. Mrs. Roosevelt was especially appreciative of the gift, found the story "delightful," read it to her grandchildren, and invited Dahl to the White House.

The hardcover book sold for a dollar and had a dust jacket. Very few books survived with the dust jackets intact and today, the original edition often commands prices in the thousands of dollars.

An Australian edition (Ayres & James Pty. Ltd., Sydney) sold an additional 30,000 copies and a 1944 British edition (Collins Publishing London) was released roughly a year later.

All three editions are the same, with one minor difference. The U.S. edition has an image of two gremlins cutting into the tail wing of a plane on the back cover. The other two editions have a blank back cover.

The book was an obvious success, but the wartime paper shortage prevented its further reprinting, which frustrated Dahl. There had been plans to do a second printing of 25,000 more copies of the American edition, but Lucille Ogle wrote to Dahl on December 7, 1943, to inform him that no additional copies would be printed.

An upset Dahl immediately wrote to Walt hoping he would be able to use his influence to change this decision. Walt replied in a letter dated December 18, 1943:

> The information given you by Lucille Ogle that the Gremlin book is out of print because of the paper shortage, I know nothing about.
>
> However, rest assured whenever there is any accounting due you for the sale of this book such revenue will be sent to you promptly. For future information on this matter, I am turning your letter over to Roy, who handles all such items, and he will answer you more completely on this point.

A review in the *New York Herald Tribune Weekly Book Review* for July 18, 1943, stated:

> Walt Disney bases a motion picture on this story. He couldn't do better.

The book established Dahl as a writer rather than just a war hero, and he was now more likely to be introduced as an author. He never considered *Gremlins* a children's book and was a bit embarassed by the attention given to it because he felt it was just a trifle. He understood that it was not an actual book, but merely something to promote the upcoming Disney film.

According to research by Disney historian David Lesjak, an article in the May 1,1943, *Daily Sentinel* newspaper published in Rome, New York, stated:

> The original manuscript for the book...[was] presented to the New York State Historical Association by the Artists' and Writers' Guild.

The manuscript was signed by Dahl and was to be displayed for several weeks in the "Gremlin Center" in Cooperstown (the museum of the New York State Historical Association) before being permanently placed in the association's library.

In 1950, Collins Publishing (New York) published a limited reprint of *The Gremlins*. For over half a century, the book remained out-of-print, the only book written by Dahl that was never reprinted.

Dahl did ask to buy back the movie rights to the book from Disney. Roy Disney wrote back on April 24, 1945, quoting him a price of $20,000, which Dahl did not have. That price was about a third of what the Disney studio had invested.

Roy assured Dahl that he and Walt would not act like a "dog in a manger" preventing Dahl from seeking any legitimate opportunity to use the material, but that in the future, even with the war over, it might turn out to be "very useful picture material."

Apparently, Dahl was casually interested in getting back the rights to the story, but not intently interested, and never brought up the subject again, even when he easily had the money to repurchase his story.

Disney historian Brian Sibley interviewed Dahl for a BBC radio program. Dahl signed Sibley's first edition of *The Gremlins* and then playfully dated it "1943". He said he did so to "cause your executors hell when they come to sort your affairs out."

In September 2006, Dark Horse Publishing produced a faithfully restored edition entitled *The Gremlins: The Lost Walt Disney Production*. It included a lengthy introduction by film historian Leonard Maltin.

A special edition of the book was produced to commemorate the 60th anniversary of the United States Air Force in 2007. It was not available to the general public and only distributed exclusively through the Army and Air Force Exchange Service. The commemorative edition sold out at all participating AAFES locations on its first day of sale.

One of the only differences in this reprint was a short history of the book on the inside dust flap.

Before the reprint by Dark Horse Publishing, the book was notoriously difficult to obtain even in poor condition and even then at ridiculously high prices because it was a limited printing of a Disney book as well as the first book featuring the work of Roald Dahl.

It was also considered a children's book, so many tiny little hands tore into the pages or scribbled on them in pencil or crayon, and as a result, not many copies survived through the decades.

CHAPTER TEN

Gremlin Concerns

Even the Disney studio itself was not immune to the "gremlin mania" that swept the country, with people claiming that any mishap must be the work of unseen gremlins.

Storyman Jim Bodrero wrote in *Dispatch from Disney's*, an in-house publication shipped to Disney personnel serving in the armed forces, that:

> Ever since work started on Flight Lieut. "Stalky" Dahl's Gremlin story, complaints are heard that the Gremlins have moved into Disney's—reports of movieola Gremlins, sound Gremlins, splice-cutting Gremlins and Monday-morning-stomach Gremlins have filtered down the corridors.
>
> To put an end to all these rumors, the studio Gremlinologists want to remind all interested parties that there is only one way to see, feel, or, as some prefer to put it, be infested with, Gremlins—that is to be shot at while piloting or serving in the crew of a military or naval aircraft on operational duty.
>
> Flying schools have no Gremlins, nor do they appear on training planes or airliners; as for the Monday-stomach things—as everyone knows, those aren't Gremlins—they're butterflies....

Not everyone was so amused by all the gremlin attention. John Moore's article in the November 8, 1942, edition of the *London Observer* newspaper, entitled "Disney's New Target, the Gremlins of the RAF, Their Name and Nature," dryly and unfavorably commented on Walt Disney's proposed personal plans to travel to England for further research on the gremlin subject:

> It will seem strange indeed to the future historians who, unraveling the tale of our troubled times, discover that in the critical year, 1942, a distinguished American traveled five thousand miles in order to make a film about elves; elves which, admittedly, no one has seen.

Walt never took the trip, but there is no documentation that the cause was the under-current of popular irritation in England regarding the whimsical project while pilots were dropping out of the war-torn skies in flames. Regardless, the Air Ministry was deluged with inquiries about Walt's proposed trip to England, which prompted Walt to send a telegram on October 3, 1942 to Air Commodore Thornton:

> Have no definite plans for trip to England. Evidently this was picked up from a conversation wherein I expressed a desire to obtain first-hand Gremlin information. However, the pressure of work here probably won't permit my going.

> But in any event we would very much like to work with Flight Lt. Dahl. If we do *The Gremlins*, we want to do it right, and we're going to impose upon you to help us all you can. Kindest regards, Walt Disney.

A Disney press release on December 8, 1942, reported that Disney had to make "some costly changes" because of "the disapproval of British flyers over the levity with which the Gremlins were being treated in the picture."

Disney's seriousness in attempting to tell a story about gremlins was constantly being teased by others. A February 1, 1943 letter to Walt from author Rayner Heppenstall who was serving with a RAF delegation in Dayton, Ohio, stated his misgivings that the film might hurt gremlin sensitivities, with possible repercussions on the war effort—and even the studio itself.

In Hedda Hopper column in the January 31, 1943, edition of the *Chicago Tribune*, which was decorated with rough artwork from the Disney studio of gremlins, Walt defended a lighthearted approach to the subject and is quoted as saying:

> Nor must we overlook the lighter side of things. That's why we under-took to make a picture on these fantastic little spirites of the air, Gremlins, first discovered by R.A.F. flyers.

> We didn't realize when we tackled the Gremlins that we had picked on such a controversial subject and that we would have a tough time getting the right dope on them. Only by keeping in the closest touch with the British Air Ministry in Washington and with the R.A.F. pilots are we going to get the right slant on them.

> We may even have to ask an R.A.F. pilot to catch a Gremlin and ship him over to us, for the sake of accuracy. Whatever we do, we certainly will take no chances on presenting the wrong slant on these devil-may-care hobgoblins, for we wouldn't want a Spitfire flying over our studio and strafing us!

Newspaper announcements about the Disney gremlins becoming the basis for a "fascinating movie" prompted a flood of correspondence to the studio, as well as a spate of gremlin themed books.

A letter to Walt Disney dated September 20, 1942, from Dahl's convoy companion, Douglas Bisgood outlined strongly his claims to the characters, including his belief that terms like fifinellas and widgets were "family names which I claim as being my originals," and announced his intention to write his own book about gremlins:

> Dear Mr. Disney, I learn with keen interest that you are making a film on "Gremlins," but being the "arch gremlin" I view with dismay the fact (if the press is correct) that you are using family names which I claim as being my originals and which I am in fact at the moment using in a book I am writing on the "Gremlin Family."
>
> It may be that Flight Lieut. R. Dahl has mentioned these titles to you as I discussed them with him when I was on my way to Canada this year. I am not so much perturbed at the monetary consideration as I am at my titles being used without any reference to myself.
>
> I am enclosing a copy of a letter which I have already sent to Dahl, which speaks for itself. It might interest you to know that I am considered an authority on "Gremlins" and it has been my pet theme for a very long time. I hope that your new film will be successful as the others, but I do feel that I have a very definite claim on the family titles you propose using. Sincerely, Douglas Bisgood.

Bisgood also wrote to Dahl, on September 18, 1942, to remind him of the shipboard exchange where he amused Dahl with his version of the gremlin story.

There was a noticeable edge in the tone of the letter where Bisgood jokingly compared Dahl's cushy attaché job in America with Bisgood's current situation where he had voluntarily quit his job training new pilots and had returned to service in his fighter squadron. (Bisgood had even recently been awarded the Distinguished Flying Cross, although he didn't mention it in the letter.)

> My Dear Roald, It may surprise you to hear from the Arch Gremlin who is at the moment in England.... I say, old boy, what's all this about Walt Disney and the Gremlins? I read in the *Times* that he is making a film of the little fellas ... what careless talk have you been up to? Apparently my advice as the Arch Gremlin was not picked—you seem to have got it all taped, but who originated the chaps?
>
> The names of Fifinella, Widget and Flippertygibbet are my own private property. Surely, old boy, the name of Bissie should appear in the film somewhere.... I hope you have made a good story out of it, but don't forget that I shall take an extremely dim view of it if my name doesn't figure somewhere. It's not that I want my name in print, as

that I am very seriously perturbed at the thoughts of Algy's relations, Fifinella, Widget and Flippertygibbet, being incorrectly portrayed.

Consider the dreadful consequences if relations became strained between the commonwealth of the pilot world and the Gremlin hierarchy. The only way to put this right would be to call in some competent consultant. Who can this be? Who knows the little fellows? Of course, I am not suggesting that you send a Catalina MK.II to fetch me, but you must agree that some action on parallel lines is vital. Yours sincerely, Douglas.

Walt, of course, had been operating under the assumption that while the general concept of gremlins was part of the RAF mythology, the particulars of the story including the unique names were solely Dahl's creation.

Even with so many other claimants of Gremlin authority suddenly appearing, Walt was still willing to give Dahl the benefit of the doubt that Flight Lieut. Bisgood was just another pilot wishing to jump on the bandwagon since Dahl had not shared with Walt the story of that Atlantic crossing where Bisgood and Dahl exchanged gremlin stories.

Walt wrote to Dahl on October 1, 1942:

> I have a letter from Flight Lieut. Douglas Bisgood in which he enclosed copy of his letter to you. I am answering him and copy of my reply is enclosed. If you have any feeling that this fellow may be inclined to cause trouble, I believe it would be wise to straighten it out now, but I may be unnecessarily concerned about the matter.
>
> However, with a thing of this sort it is natural to expect a certain amount of jealousy, but nevertheless when we undertake the production of a film, the cost of which runs into many thousands of dollars, we must surround ourselves with every precautionary measure. I would appreciate your reactions to this particular situation.

Walt's letter to Bisgood dated October 1, 1942, stated:

> I am glad to know of your interest and the part you have played in connection with the Gremlins. However, I don't want you to be too severe with Flight Lieut. Dahl. Frankly, I do not believe he has misrepresented anything to us. He has been very unselfish in his attitude toward the whole matter. He has presented the Gremlins as a collection of stories and incidents that have sprung up with the boys in the R.A.F.
>
> The deal we are consummating with Flight Lieut. Dahl for the use of these characters is one where the royalties go to the Benevolent Fund of the R.A.F., so you see it is not entirely a personal thing with him. It has the full cooperation of the British Air Ministry, and

Commander Thornton of the British Embassy in Washington has entered into the project.

It is our hope that this film will help to bring about a better understanding between the British and American people. We hope, too, that our screen treatment of the Gremlins will meet with your personal approval and that you will look upon it with pride in knowing that you, as one of the R.A.F. boys, have contributed your share to Gremlin-lore. Sincerely, Walt.

Dahl tried to calm Walt's confusion and anxiety in a letter dated October 7, 1942, that read in part:

I know Bissie very well and have many a time discussed gremlins with him; he is without doubt an eminent Gremlinologist. I do not think, however, that you need take anything he says too seriously and I am quite sure that he will not cause any trouble.

More particularly when he finds out how we are treating the matter and what we are doing with the proceeds.

Perhaps because profits were earmarked for the R.A.F. Benevolent Fund, Bisgood never did cause any trouble or send any further communication. He died soon after the war.

October 14 brought a letter from literary agent Barthold Fles offering the Disney studio the opportunity to purchase the rights to another book, *David and the Gremlins*, by British writer, R. Sugden Tilley.

One of the most stubborn claimants was Charles Graves, who had authored in April 1941 a history of the RAF entitled *The Thin Blue Line, or Adventures in the RAF*. He claimed he was the first person to have mentioned gremlins in print and was gathering more material on the subject for a sequel to his book.

He argued that Disney should give him monetary compensation so that he could pay the three RAF pilots who had shared gremlin stories with him for his book. His request was for 500 guineas (approximately $2,100 in those days) and he emphasized he was being so adamant in his demand only for the benefit of the three RAF pilots.

E.J. Davis, who worked for Walt Disney Mickey Mouse Ltd. in London, wrote to Roy Disney on October 8, 1942:

I have been able to contact Charles Graves; he has been out of town for the past two weeks, but he called in at the office yesterday and I had a long talk with him. According to Mr. Graves, the Gremlin legend first saw the light in 1923 but did not develop until the war; as a matter of fact it is only in the last nine months or a year that these fortunate figures have really become more widely known.

Gremlins first appeared in print in *The Thin Blue Line*. This book was written by Charles Graves at the request of the Air Ministry and was published on April 17, 1941, by Hutchinson. It was widely read by members of the RAF as well as the public and the reference to Gremlins resulted in a big development of the legend.

Recently, Graves has been going round the country visiting R.A.F. Stations and collecting stories about Gremlins for a new book to be published early in 1943, and having seen publicity regarding a proposed Disney Gremlin film, he believes that the material he has collected together with drawings and photographs and any future material would be of use to you in the making of this film.

The question of price arose and Graves named a figure of 500 guineas for the material he has at present, pointing out that this sum would have to be divided between sundry other persons who had helped him to collect it. He also stated that he would be quite willing to put into writing that Disney might use the material in any way he chose.

Some of the drawings, he said, might be very amateurish but they might help as a background for the creation of the Disney Gremlins. Perhaps you will let me know as soon as possible whether you can use Charles Graves' material at the price he named; he considers he has at present about two-thirds of all the material there is to be collected on this subject in this country.

Graves refused to be placated until he was convinced to drop the matter after receiving a stern letter from the Air Ministry on May 22, 1943, that reminded him that all gremlin revenue from non-film items such as books and character merchandise would be donated to the RAF Benevolent Fund.

Dahl sent a letter to Walt to reinforce that Graves would not be a problem. In a letter dated May 22, 1943, Dahl wrote:

You will remember that when I was last with you, you gave me a letter which Roy had received from your people in London regarding a certain Charles Graves who was holding out for a lot of money and was claiming a lot of copyrights.

Roy, in his note to you, said that you would probably have to get him on your side. I took the matter up with Air Ministry where, as a matter of fact, we have recruited some very prominent lawyers from civil life.

A pretty strong letter was sent to Mr. Graves stating that the Air Ministry had heard it being said that Graves was proposing to blackmail you into paying him cash for his Gremlin story, thereby deliberately doing down the R.A.F. Benevolent Fund in an indirect way. The letter added that it was hoped that this was not true and would be glad of his confirmation in writing that he had no such intention and that any stories to this effect were lies.

Apparently, Graves was away at the time, but the letter produced an immediate effect on his return in the shape of three agitated phone calls. His story was that he was doing it for three R.A.F. men who had given him the dope and that he did not see why they should not get something out of it. He was told to think again.

The latest position is that he is thoroughly rattled and that Air Ministry doubts very much whether he will pursue the matter any further. They are going to try to pin him down further and will report the progress. Your people in London are being informed so that they also can take a firm line. I am attaching a copy of this letter for Roy and think it safe to say that he need not worry himself any more about it. The matter is in good hands. Yours very sincerely, Stalky.

Dahl sent another letter to Walt on July 9, 1943:

I don't think that you need to trouble any more about the man called Charles Graves who was making trouble for you in London and asking for money, as he claimed copyright on the Gremlin idea. He has now written to the Air Ministry saying that if they think it is undesirable that anybody should be paid there is nothing that he can do about it.

He says that he disclaims any intention of making money himself and he tells them that they can use the letter he sends them in any way they please. It may interest you to know that he informs Air Ministry that Rex Armour had said to him that "there would be no difficulty giving him a WROTE among the screen credits" which seemed to me to have been what may have caused some of the trouble.

It was Graves in his book that first suggested in print the name gremlin referred to a goblin that had crawled out of a Fremlins beer bottle so that the word was a combination of the words goblin and Fremlin.

Others have suggested that some unnamed airman who was either reading or thinking about *Grimm's Fairy Tales* while drinking Fremlins combined the words Grimm with Fremlin.

While the fact that revenue from the Disney Dahl project would go to the RAF Benevolent Fund seemed to quell the claims of others, it did not prevent gremlins from appearing in other books around this same time.

Several books, including *Sh! Gremlins* by "H.W.," *Gremlins on the Job* by Judy Vargam, *Listen Hitler! The Gremlins Are Coming* by Inez Hogan, and *The Gremlins of Lieut. Oggins* by Irwin Shapiro, were published but did not receive wide distribution, perhaps due to paper shortages at the time, or not much publicity, and are not remembered today.

Making matters worse, these books and several magazine articles had created artwork of their version of what gremlins looked like while the Disney studio continued to struggle to nail down their concept.

One of the reasons Walt had pushed for the publication of Dahl's story in *Cosmopolitan* was to see if he would flush out any other claimants to the gremlins. None appeared.

However, Walt's concerns increased that he no longer had control over the characters or their story, and definitely not the name. He realized that he had to aggressively lay claim to the property before things got even more out of hand.

CHAPTER ELEVEN

Walt Disney Talks Gremlins

The British Air Ministry requested Walt write an article on gremlins for their November 16, 1942, *RAF Journal*. It was later reprinted in *Slipstream, A Royal Air Force Anthology* (1946).

A pencil notation at the top of the Disney archives copy of the article states "Ted Sears 11-16-42" and seems to indicate strongly that the talented Disney storyman may have ghostwritten this article, especially since notes from "Ted" to Walt dated November and early December of 1942 indicate that Sears was deeply involved in gathering material.

Once such note from November says:

> Collecting all possible dope on R.A.F. activities and characters in order to have a background of authentic information for anyone who may go on the Gremlin subject. Also trying out plot situations and rough outlines.

> Going through 8 or 10 of the best up to date R.A.F. books published in England and here, but all by R.A.F. men. Also keeping in touch with news and magazine articles. Bernice has the complete file. Will make notes of anything that might be of value. Ted.

Like everything from the Disney studio with Walt's name attached to it, Walt had to personally approve it and to make sure it "sounded" like him. Here is Walt's article:

> As soon as the Air Ministry heard that I was about to do a Gremlin film, they asked me to write a short article expressing my views of Gremlins in general.

> Now I don't think this is a fair request. Truthfully, I have no more idea of Gremlins than I have of fighter tactics or high level bombing. I can only go by what I hear.

> I consider it one of the great misfortunes of my life that not being an air gunner, a pilot, or a navigator I shall never be able to boast of having seen a Gremlin in person.

I shall never be able to discuss, as you men do, the deeper and more subtle points of Gremlin-lore, and suggest new methods of training them to behave. Unfortunately, I am not a Gremlinologist.

With every other film I've made, I've been able, in times of discussion, to stand up and shout "You're wrong!" and then proceed to back up my argument with detailed specifications regarding the size and color of the noses of the Seven Dwarfs, the shape of Pinocchio's hat, or the length of Bambi's legs.

But in dealing with your Gremlins, I'll admit I'm at a loss. I can't even pretend that I've seen one, and I must get all of my information and instruction from the R.A.F. fliers themselves.

Numbers of them have passed through here and have come to see me and tried to help me. And from their careful descriptions I have tried to draw the Gremlin as he is actually seen by you in his various phases, on your machines in the air, and as you see him around the airdrome and in the mess.

No one realizes more than I the importance of these little men and the task I am undertaking.

So far I haven't a clue.

That's why I'm depending upon you men for all the Gen I can possibly get about Gremlins. As you can see, I've even begun to pick up some of your language. (Note: Pukka gen was R.A.F. slang for "the real low-down.")

Naturally, I can't place the entire responsibility upon your shoulders, but I do wish you'd keep me informed of any new tactics and habits the Gremlins develop from time to time.

Do you suppose it would be possible to find one of the little fellows who could be spared and have him crated and shipped to California? I can assure you that he'll be treated with the utmost care and consideration at this end. We have a plentiful supply of used postage stamps of all vintages, which I understand is his staple diet, and he would be allowed the freedom of the Studio. Although I wouldn't be able to see him, I'm sure he'd serve as an excellent Technical Advisor.

Perhaps this is asking for the impossible, but I do intend to see that when the Gremlins reach the screen, they will be the same Gremlins that you men have flown with and lived with.

And if I should put any blacks in this film due to lack of Pukka gen, I do hope you won't tear me off a terrific strip.

Walt Disney

Roald Dahl wrote to Walt in a letter dated December 2, 1942:

> I have just received a telegram from Air Ministry, asking me to convey to you their thanks for sending along the article on Gremlins for the *R.A.F. Journal*, which they happily received on time. They said it was just what they wanted and seemed very pleased about it all.
>
> I, myself, Walt also want to thank you and all those in the Studio for the extremely pleasant time, which you gave me during my short visit, and especially Jim [Bodrero]. I must say that never in my life have I seen so many "good types" as we call them, all gathered under one roof. I haven't enjoyed myself so much for ages. Many thanks for everything. Yours very sincerely, Stalky.

Walt did have sincere anxiety about wanting to portray the RAF mythology of the Gremlins as authentically as possible. This article was a legitimate plea for input from those who were intimately involved with Gremlins, since Dahl was not being much help other than discouraging any attempts that were made.

Everyone seemed to have an opinion about gremlins and how they should be portrayed, and it wasn't just the RAF pilots.

Nelson Poynter who, during World War II, formed the U.S. Information Agency (sometimes called the Office of War Information) sent a short note on October 9, 1942, to Joe Grant who was working in the character model department at the Disney studio:

> Dear Joe;
>
> If you develop the Gremlin idea, I respectfully suggest that you should show these heroic little democrats as having a dynamic rather than a static society. Their life in the forest need not have been an isolate one. They are peace-loving, but not saps.
>
> They have preferred to make consumer goods and dedicate their energies to science and progress rather than militarism. But when they are disturbed, when their way of life is threatened, they prove to be resourceful, albeit, unprepared. They are fighting for the continued opportunity to progress.
>
> Sincerely, Nels

Walter Winchell was a hugely influential newspaper columnist, often writing blurbs of celebrity gossip eagerly read and believed by countless readers. Occasionally, he would have a guest writer if he was away on some business.

He allowed Walt (or someone at the Disney studio writing under Walt's byline) to write the column on December 28, 1942, to promote Disney's upcoming film. The column was accompanied by four black-and-white illustrations by Bill Justice.

The first featured two gremlins (the one who is sitting looks like Gremlin Gus) drilling a hole into an airplane wing, the second had two widgets (one floating on its back), the third had a full figure of a fifinella bowing, and the final illustration was of a gremlin and a fifinella astride a bullet in flight.

BATTING FOR WINCHELL

Lt. Com. Walter Winchell of the U.S. Navy is temporarily unable to produce his column, which is being handled by guest columnists:

"Pukka Gen* on Gremlins" by Walt Disney (*RAF slang for "the real low-down")

Ever seen a real Gremlin? No? Well, maybe it's because you haven't been up in a British Spitfire swapping bullets with a Messerschmitt, or dodging German flak in a bombing raid over Hamburg.

RAF fighter pilots and members of bomber crews who have seen real action are the only ones eligible to see real Gremlins.

Of course, lots of others think they've seen them, but they've only seen the imitations: Gound Wallopers the pilots call them.

Ever since the Gremlins were discovered, the press has been deluged with drawings of grotesque hobgoblins, bearded dwarfs, misshapen elves, pixies, spooks and what-not, all trying to pass themselves off as Gremlins.

But don't let them kid you. The real Gremlins, discovered by the RAF, are a distinctively individual race; and are by no means ugly. They have their own original characteristics, and bear no resemblance to the outlandish monstrosities and gruesome nightmares cooked up by artists of the past.

How are we going to make a picture and write a book about them if we can't see them?

That's where we get a real break. Thanks to the British air ministry, all the RAF pilots who have seen Gremlins have promised to give us first-hand information on them.

They've already supplied us with plenty of Gen to get started on, and letters are coming in every day filled with blow-by-blow accounts of the latest contacts with these remarkable little guys. The general consensus is that they're less than a foot high and built on the chunky side. They wear zippered flying suits and their horns grow right thru their helmets.

Some affect green bowler hats and all have black suction-boots for walking on wings at 300 miles an hour.

After all, the RAF feels responsible for its Gremlins and wants them pictured just as they really are. And that puts us on a spot. They warned us that if we fall down on the job or put up any blacks they'd take a dim view of our efforts and probably tear us off a colossal strip, which we assume means pinning our ears back.

Only last month the British embassy sent one of the foremost Gremlinologists out to the studio; a flight lieutenant who has been on speaking terms with every known type of Gremlin.

He put us straight on lots of things. We found out, for instance, that Gremlins never operate higher than 30,000 feet. It's the Spandules who take over above this altitude.

They hang on to the leading edge of your wing and slowly exhale, forming a nice thick coating of ice. Spandules are flat rug-like individuals covered with fur and have large pockets for storing hailstones, which they chew constantly.

From all reports, the Fifinella (that's the female Gremlin) is a honey. They tell us her face is fizzing and she has wizard curves, all in the proper places. Nothing ropey about this little crumpet. We gather from this that she's really an eyeful.

The boys tell us that you'll never catch a Fifinella drilling holes in your wing, cutting your parachute straps or draining the alcohol from your compass. All a Fifinella has to do is hop aboard a plane for a joyride and the Gremlins will follow her in droves. (Statistics show one Fifinella to every 12 Gremlins.)

By the time they've chased her back and forth from one wing-tip to the other, wiggling your wing flaps, swinging on your aerial wire and playing see-saw on your elevators, you'll wish she'd stayed at home to mind the Widgets.

Widgets? They're the new born Gremlins that appear in nests hidden in the dark corners of your aircraft. In every batch of Widgets you'll find a Flibberty-gibbet. She's the one who eventually becomes a Fifinella. Before they're a day old, Widgets are up to mischief.

They have very high baby voices and chatter incessantly. Since they're not equipped with suction boots like older Gremlins, they usually concentrate on the instrument board and have a marvellous time putting all the gauges out of whack.

The fact that Gremlins have become so real and play such an important role in the thoughts and conversations of the flyers is really a tribute to the courage, morale and sense of humor of the RAF.

And when the gong sounds ending the final round of the war, the chances are that the Gremlins will be entitled to a large slice of credit for making their appearance during England's darkest hour and carrying on in their mischievous way until victory was certain.

Despite his respect and affection for Walt, Dahl had great fun playing on Walt's worries like a cat with a mouse, especially since he was a little resentful that the media was assuming that Walt was an expert on Gremlins.

Dahl continued to allude to Gremlin behavior, appearance, and characteristics without ever finally defining them for the Disney staff, so that whenever the Disney staff did anything with the project, there was always some type of disappointed commentary from Dahl.

In "Gremlins…A Warning," an article in the April 10, 1943, edition of the *Chicago News*, Dahl wrote:

> Although we seldom mention Gremlins outside our own airdromes, a few months ago some of us wrote a story or two about them. We even went so far as to take Walt Disney into our confidence and agree to his making a film, but only after convincing ourselves that he would not let his imagination run away with him and that he would not pretend he could see them when, of course, he couldn't.

> We made him promise that he would depict Gremlins exactly as they are and as we see them; and we in turn promised to tell him accurately just how they looked. But neither in our stories nor in talking to Walt did we tell everything.

> When these stories were published, people all over American began claiming that they had seen Gremlins! Some even went so far as to say that they had seen Fifinellas or Widgets…. Perhaps this was all our fault. We should have made it quite clear that only men who fly can ever hope to see these small creatures, that they rarely associate themselves with anything not directly concerned with airplanes or airdromes.

> Nevertheless, the legend grew. We heard with surprise that Gremlins were supposed to be puncturing tires and hiding collar studs, or putting seeds in seedless raisins and stains on stainless steel, or a hundred other wild and ludicrous things.

Dahl loved being in control and he felt undervalued by the RAF top brass. He felt he had not been shown the proper respect and appreciation for handling Disney as he had. He felt he had brought wide attention and soon some much-needed revenue to the RAF.

On the other hand, his superiors found him to be too casual with necessary formalities, bordering on insubordination. Some felt that he leveraged his good looks and charm in place of any genuine diplomatic skills. His growing list of sexual conquests, including the prominent Clare Booth Luce, supposedly to obtain access to information, was much a subject of concern.

Some even felt that the gremlin project was more of an irritation and an embarrassment rather than a benefit and needed to be resolved quickly and Dahl once again consigned to a lower rung in the larger scheme of things instead of partying in southern California.

Dahl was informed by friends that his attitude and behavior had made him some powerful enemies and he needed to watch his back.

Clement Caines, an assistant under secretary in the Air Department, wrote that Dahl's story was all just a "joke" and that the Air Ministry should distance itself from the project and deny Disney to describe the film as being "sponsored or approved by the Air Council or the Air Ministry."

Caines also wrote to the Air Ministry that they should put together a document so that, in the event of Dahl's death, the RAF would continue to receive any benefits from the book and movie.

When Dahl found out, he was incensed, feeling that his generosity and integrity were being impugned and that he was being accused of trying to "embezzle any of the money which I had promised to give away," as he wrote to his mother.

Dahl was sharp enough to sense this resentment from his higher-ups and so he may have acted out a bit when dealing with Walt about gremlins to reinforce that he was the one in control and that his authority needed to be respected.

Others who offered alternate views about gremlins needed to be dismissed since Dahl was the only true expert. Dahl was not adverse to trotting out the RAF and the Air Ministry as boogeymen who were even more displeased that Dahl's guidance was not being followed to the letter by Disney.

Dahl wrote a defiant article for the March 1943 issue of *This Week* magazine where he begged readers to "treat (gremlins) with respect" and that all non-RAF versions were impostors and fakes. He once again emphasized that only those who flew could see them, "but NO-ONE ELSE."

While trying to be respectful and genuinely liking Dahl as a person, Walt, who also liked to be in complete control, responded by bringing to the studio other RAF pilots to share their stories.

"Our studio became a sort of Mecca for visiting airmen," stated Walt. However, none of those visitors were in accord on anything. Walt sought input not only on *The Gremlins* but also *Victory Through Air Power* (1943).

Walt also tried to work out some type of marketing plan that would forever bind gremlins with Disney while trying to mollify Dahl.

After all, Dahl might be a self-proclaimed expert on gremlins, but Walt felt he had proven he knew what would make a great motion picture and how to market a film and its characters to continue to support the final product. Dahl, of course, had a different opinion.

CHAPTER TWELVE

Gremlin Merchandise

If Walt Disney had initially feared that one of his challenges with doing the Gremlin film was acquainting American audiences with the concept of the British gremlins, the beginning of 1943 showed that the real fear was that "Gremlin mania," as it was dubbed by the press, threatened Disney's exclusive rights to the characters.

Count Basie recorded "Dance of the Gremlins." The *New York Evening Post* reported in January 9, 1943:

> The R.A.F.'s Gremlins will become swing fodder in Count Basie's new song "Dance of the Gremlins," sub-captioned "There's a Gremlin in the Groove."

The song had no lyrics and no indication other than the title that it was Gremlins-connected in any way. It was just Basie's typical light, swinging rhythm section with Basie leading from the piano.

Obviously, the song was meant to capitalize on the public's new awareness of gremlins. At the time, Basie and his band were on the West Coast where they appeared in five different Hollywood films released within the span of a few months.

A short-lived daily comic strip drawn by Dorman Smith for the NEA syndicate entitled "The Gremlins" ran from January 4 through May 15, 1943. In a telegram to the Disney studio dated January 8, 1943, Dahl wrote that he was worried about whether Walt was "doing anything about the comic strip."

Fashionable ladies began wearing "Gremlin Hats" while still more magazine and newspaper articles and references to gremlins began to flood the American consciousness, threatening to move gremlins into the public domain. Other animation studios were registering titles for possible Gremlin short animated cartoons to try to capitalize on the mania.

There were even companies other than Disney developing Gremlin merchandise, as evidenced by this letter from Antoinette Spitzer to Disney merchandise executive Kay Kamen dated November 2, 1942:

> Lord & Taylor started working on Gremlin merchandise (their own conception of Gremlins, of course) six months ago, and they are planning to do a whole Christmas campaign on it. Their Gremlin is their own design idea, not based on [the] Walt Disney picture.
>
> Since they are going ahead on this promotion and since we can't do anything to supply them with merchandise they have their own—it just occurred to me that we might get in on it in a publicity way; however, should you make a tie-up with another store...."

Something needed to be done quickly and firmly to establish Disney's rights to gremlins.

It was animator Bill Justice who designed the character of Gremlin Gus who was the leader of these mischievous creatures of the air. Gus, in his red flight suit, flight helmet with goggles, thick gloves, brown derby hooked askew on one of his horns, scraggly white mustache, and stout figure was hugely appealing. He was a fatherly or grandfatherly character, but still seemed full of mischief.

An official Disney studio memo was sent down to those involved in the Dahl project to push the character of Gremlin Gus in all publicity and drawings in an effort to establish that particular gremlin as an exclusive Disney property that could be copyrighted and trademarked.

Kay Kamen arranged for a variety of products to be marketed quickly, including the addition of a series of stories about Gremlin Gus in one of the highest selling monthly comic books of all time, *Walt Disney's Comics and Stories* from Western Publishing.

A one-page illustration of Gremlin Gus adapted from Walt Kelly's comic book work in *Walt Disney Comics and Stories* pops up mysteriously in *The Walt Disney Paint Book*, a coloring book from Whitman published in 1944. It is the only gremlin drawing in the book which is otherwise filled with drawings of Mickey, Donald, and others, obviously adapted as well from comic book panels.

Kamen had joined the Disney studio in 1932 and brought much-needed income to the company through his savvy merchandising of the Disney characters. Walt trusted him to work his business connection magic with the gremlins.

Another effort to establish the Disney version of gremlin characters was the creation of a limited number of stuffed dolls.

In 1930, Charlotte Clark made the first Mickey Mouse stuffed doll, but the public demand for the quality item exceeded her ability, even with a team of seamstresses to produce them. She then supplied designs of Disney character dolls to the Knickerbocker Toy Company, which took over making the dolls, and later the Gund Manufacturing Company.

Even when Kamen started licensing the making of stuffed Disney character dolls and Clark's "Doll House" on Hyperion Avenue that operated near the studio had long since closed, Clark continued to design stuffed toys for the company to use as promotional products through the 1940s and 1950s. Walt often displayed them in his office and gave them as gifts to celebrities and media.

Her work is fairly distinctive and emphasizes rounded shapes, wide eyes, and of course, attention to detail. She had just finished doing dolls from *Saludos Amigos* like Jose Carioca when she was given the assignment to create gremlin dolls for publicity purposes.

Clark produced dolls based on the Disney designs for gremlins, fifinellas, and widgets, and there are several existing photos of Walt and Dahl posing happily with the dolls. The cloth widget doll was produced in two different sizes and at least three different colors: red, blue, and grey.

In May 1943, Dahl had sent to Walt a request for twelve of the widget dolls, even offering to pay. Walt sent the dolls with a note saying he didn't want Dahl to pay because Walt "prefers to keep the 'Gremlinologist' indebted" to him.

In a December 18, 1943, telegram, Dahl asked:

> Very special request for a Fifinella Doll and two Widgets, but especially Fifinella. Are there any chance any around? If so, most grateful. Send airmail.

Walt responded on December 20:

> Terribly sorry, but there isn't a Fifinella on the place. Widgets, yes—in fact, they have sold so very well that Mrs. Clark (the lady who personally makes all of our dolls) has been devoting all of her time to Widgets for the past several weeks.

> At no time have we ever had more than just a few Fifinellas—they didn't sell well so we discontinued making them. However, three Widgets were air expressed to you today. Best Christmas Greetings—Sincerely, Walt.

The cover of the May 1943 issue of *Playthings* magazine (the national magazine of the toy trade at the time) announced "Walt Disney's Gremlins of the R.A.F." and featured on the cover a puzzled fighter pilot whose Hurricane fighter is infested by a widget, a fifinella, and a gremlin (who is drilling holes in the right wing). A small box at the side stated:

> Like all Walt Disney characters, Walt Disney "Gremlins" are authentic. The definition of "authentic" is—"having a genuine origin or authority." That origin or authority is the R.A.F. All drawings, all titles, all scripts are fully covered by U.S. and foreign copyrights. All rights

reserved. Walt Disney GREMLINS offer unusual opportunities for merchandising tie-ups. For further information write or call: KAY KAMEN representing Walt Disney Productions.

The Character Novelty Company (a Disney licensee from 1940–1947) manufactured a widget hand puppet in at least three different colors: pink, yellow, and grey. The puppet, which was produced in 1943, originally sold for $1.50 with a paper tag that read:

> This is an exclusive Walt Disney design of one of the famous Gremlin characters discovered by the R.A.F.

"A Walt Disney Picture Puzzle" from the Jaymar company in 1943 had over 300 pieces showcasing a color illustration of eleven gremlins, one widget, and one fifinella attacking an Allied fighter plane with the addition of left and right vertical margins featuring characters from the then un-produced film.

Disney licensee W.L. Stensgaard and Associates created several full-sized gremlins figures constructed out of papier-mâché. One set was used by the Dayton Company, a fur storage company in Minneapolis, Minnesota. The display with a sign stating "The Gremlin Fur Destruction Committee" featured four three-dimensional gremlins figures doing mischief to furs.

On May 26, 1943, Stensgaard himself wrote to Bennett Cerf, the editor at Random House, which had published *The Gremlins*, about the possible use of the figures to help promote the book in stores, including a photograph of the display:

> The Gremlin Fur Destruction Committee is a series of four full relief Gremlins figures. The display is four feet high overall and about forty-two inches in diameter. These Gremlins are made of papier-mâché, hand painted heads with very colorful costumes.
>
> This display was sold or rented to certain stores in connection with their fur storage and repair promotion plans. For instance, the Dayton Company of Minneapolis, one of America's finest stores, purchased one of these and is using it very effectively. They have also used certain of the characters in their advertising promotion on the same subject.
>
> Of course the stores can use this Gremlin series in many situations, aside from Fur Storage.

Kamen was in the process of arranging other merchandising deals utilizing the characters when the word came that the project had been cancelled. He later died in an airplane crash in 1949.

Decades later, Dark Horse Publishing would produce new Gremlin merchandise based on the vintage Disney designs.

CHAPTER THIRTEEN

The Life-Saver Controversy

Another way the Disney studio attempted to secure all rights to the Disney version of the gremlins characters was by licensing them to appear in a full-color, full-page magazine ad for Mint O Green, Spear Mint, and Pep O Mint Life Savers that appeared in *LOOK* magazine in 1943.

Life Savers were a ring-shaped hard candy meant as a summer candy that wouldn't melt in the heat like chocolate. Its name was derived from the fact that the individual pieces looked like life preservers used on ships, a circle with a hole in the middle.

The candy was created in 1912 by Clarence Crane who sold the registered trademark to Edward John Noble, the founder of the Life Savers and Candy Company in 1913. Several different mint and fruit flavors have been introduced over the years, but the familiar five-flavor roll first appeared in 1935.

Amazingly, during World War II (when this Disney ad appeared), other candy manufacturers had donated their sugar rations to keep Life Savers in production so that the little candies could be shared with soldiers overseas.

Not only did the candy survive being shipped, especially to tropic zones, better than chocolate, it was a small package that reminded those serving in the military of memories of home.

During the war years, the company supplied 23 million boxes of Life Savers to the armed forces. Rolls of Life Savers were packed into the American G.I. field ration kits.

This use of the Gremlins in the approximately 13.5" x 10.25" Life-Saver advertisement would help introduce the Disney designs of the characters to the public and hopefully build anticipation for the forthcoming film as well as associating those characters with a beloved treat.

A copyright for Walt Disney Productions was to the lower-right side of the illustration, confirming Disney's ownership of these particular Gremlins. In addition, the ad produced some unexpected but appreciated licensing revenue that could be used to offset the mounting production costs of the film.

The top two-thirds of the page had an illustration (with Walt Disney's famous signature in the lower right) featuring a dozen colorful gremlins, fifinellas, and widgets desperately running away from gigantic rolling Life Savers (red, yellow, orange, and green) and toward the reader, with a few of them flattened by the candy treats.

The text for the advertisement read:

> GREMLIN CHASERS. You've heard of the Gremlins...pesky little troublemakers that hang around air fields...army camps...ports of call...and battle stations. One good antidote for Gremlins is LIFE SAVERS...they cheer a fellow up when the Gremlins get him down.
>
> Maybe that's why our armed forces are ordering so many of them... so...if you have trouble getting some favorite flavor...blame it on the Gremlins.

The ad prompted Dahl, who was becoming even more difficult in regard to how Disney was handling his Gremlins, in a letter dated May 19, 1943, to protest about the possible damage to the mystique of the characters being used in such an obvious commercial way:

> I nearly fell off my chair when I opened *LOOK* magazine this morning and saw the Life Saver advertisement with our Gremlins in it. Imagine then my horror at finding a group of the little men, not to mention the Widgets and the Fifinellas, busily engaged in playing around with a lot of over-sized and bilious looking peppermint life savers!
>
> I was horrified not only because the Gremlins were being completely misrepresented, but also because I could see you destroying in the eyes of the public the legend around which you are going to build your film, and upon which the success of the whole movie will depend. We hope to infuse a certain mystic quality into the film, and in order to achieve this we must try to avoid Pep O Mint and Wint O Green Tablets.
>
> Please do not think that I do not realize that you depend to a great extent for your revenue upon advertising rights and that it is essential for you to make use of this medium if you are going to make any profits out of the deal, but surely you realize that if the public are going to see Gremlins playing with peppermints, hitching up bicycles, trying out tooth brushes, and telling the people that if they use Listerine Antiseptic, they will not get dandruff in their hair, then I think, in fact I am convinced, that the legend will be ruined.
>
> You see, people are beginning to regard you as an authority on these things, which is as it should be because you are rapidly becoming one through the medium of your advisers; therefore, anything you say about Gremlins from now on, goes.

I suggest that you give very serious consideration to the following: that the use of Gremlins in advertising should, where possible, be confined solely to aircraft manufacturers or to makers of aircraft parts, and that the things you make them do in your pictures should be the things which they normally do anyway. This will preserve the whole idea.

If financial considerations make it impossible for you to narrow down the sales of advertising rights to this extent, then the makers of peppermint tablets, gum and toothpaste will have to have an airplane, a real well-drawn airplane, embodied in their advertisements if they wish to utilize Gremlins.

And on this airplane the Gremlins can be shown going about their business. I can see that there might well be difficulties over this, but surely it is the only way of dealing with the matter and of preserving the true character of the story.

I am sorry to be a nuisance over all of this, but I am quite sure that not only you, but Jim [Bodereo] and Ted [Sears], and others working on the subject will know how I feel and what the R.A.F. would think; so could you please let me have your reactions by return.

Between us I am sure that we can come to some arrangement. Yours very sincerely, Stalky.

Walt very patiently reassured Dahl that it was all just part of the process to establish copyright in a reply dated May 26, 1943:

Your letter of May 19th received and contents noted. You may rest assured that any suggestions you have will always be given careful consideration. A copy of your letter is being sent to my brother Roy and Mr. Kay Kamen in New York. However, I would like to correct an impression which was indicated in your letter.

It is not the financial returns with which we are concerned, but through this medium we are able to establish our rights to characters through various forms of publication, and unless these rights are established, we may not have any control over the Gremlins when they do come out. Our entire idea is one to establish our copyrights with no thought whatever of financial gain.

I think you better have a talk with Mr. Kamen and Roy as I believe you have the wrong impression of just how we function. We have reached a point in the story where, I believe, it would be helpful if you could make arrangements to come out for a period of at least two months so that, together, we can whip the story into its final shape.

If you are not able to do this, I do not feel that I can be held responsible to the Royal Air Force for the finished treatment of this material.

> Therefore, I wish you would please do what you can to come to the studio for at least the time necessary to put the script into shape for production. I would appreciate knowing what the possibilities are for you to spend some time with us.

Dahl was unable to make arrangements to visit the Disney studios to work on the treatment. By now, he was having to use his own unpaid leave to do so, which he was reluctant to do, and felt trapped.

Kamen wrote to Roy Disney on June 1, 1943:

> I just called Lt. Dahl long-distance and had a nice chat and explained to him that I didn't believe that the proper understanding existed about the way in which we have to handle Walt Disney subjects for the purposes of protection and for other reasons, and that it was quite difficult to handle the subject in a long-distance telephone conversation.
>
> Basically when the operator asks you to limit it to 5 minutes, and that it was also quite impossible to handle the subject by correspondence, and that I thought it would be nice for him and me to have a visit either in Washington or New York quite soon.
>
> Dahl agreed with all of this and was very nice and I am quite sure that we will get together in a few days and that everything will be satisfactory to him. I am sorry that he and I did not meet sooner to get to know each other, but it will straighten out in the end.

This incident was just only one of many continuing challenges between Dahl and the Disney studio about the proper presentation of gremlins that added to the film not moving along as quickly as it should have at this point.

The Gremlins was not the only project consuming time and talent at the Disney studio and these continual interruptions from Dahl were becoming disconcerting and distracting. Dahl never seemed pleased and kept demanding more, yet was not available for consultation.

CHAPTER FOURTEEN

Gremlin Comic Books

In order to establish the Disney design of gremlins, Kay Kamen made arrangements for a series of stories featuring Gremlin Gus to appear in the highest selling U.S. comic book of all time, *Walt Disney's Comics and Stories*. By the early 1950s, that title was selling a confirmed three million copies every month.

In 1933, Kamen signed the initial contract granting Western the license to exclusive book rights to all the Walt Disney characters for a series of children's publications. In 1937, Kamen negotiated for Western to take over the production and publication of *Mickey Mouse Magazine,* a popular periodical.

That magazine evolved into *Walt Disney's Comics and Stories* in October 1940. Western produced the writing and artwork for the comic book as well as other Disney comic books, but that division was financed and distributed by Dell Publishing, so the comic books are referred to as Dell Comics.

Dell's East Coast division, in New York, was headed by Oskar Lebeck, and its West Coast division, in Los Angeles, by Eleanor Packer.

Cartoonist Walt Kelly is best known as the creator of the *Pogo* newspaper comic strip, which began as a feature in Dell funny animal comic books. Starting in 1942, Kelly began writing and drawing a series of Dell comic books based on cute animal stories, fairy tales, and nursery rhymes.

Kelly had a varied career in cartooning that included working for several years at the Disney studio as a story artist and animator.

Like many artists during the Great Depression, the only place to find work was at the Disney studio in Burbank, California, which was expanding its staff rapidly to complete the first animated feature cartoon *Snow White and the Seven Dwarfs* (1937).

Kelly worked at Disney from January 6, 1936, to May 27, 1941, leaving exactly one day before the infamous strike started on an approved extended leave of absence to take care of his ailing older sister in Connecticut. However, Kelly didn't officially end his employment with the studio until September 12 of that year.

After a probationary training period that involved learning how to in-between animation drawings, Kelly was assigned to the Disney story department where he supplied gags for the shorts, including ones with Donald Duck.

However, by late 1939, Disney needed additional animators to work on its new features and Kelly willingly shifted over to the role of assistant animator for Fred Moore, an expert on drawing Mickey Mouse, and sometimes as an assistant for Ward Kimball, who told animation historian Michael Barrier:

> We loved the way he drew Mickey Mouse. His proportions were very subtly different from the model sheet and even the accredited authority for Mickey Mouse, Fred Moore, would laugh at Kelly's drawings. They were just basically funny. In fact, everything he drew was funny.

Kelly worked on the Mickey Mouse shorts *Mickey's Surprise Party* (1939), *The Little Whirlwind* (1941), and *The Nifty Nineties* (1941). He also worked on such feature films as *Pinocchio* (Gepetto inside Monstro), *Fantasia* (Bacchus riding a donkey), *Dumbo* (the ringmaster and the crows), and *The Reluctant Dragon* (the little boy).

Kelly felt constricted by animation and had not received the necessary additional training before entering the story department, so his animation artwork was rough and required clean-up by others. He also had difficulty remaining "on model" with characters, usually adding some slight personal artistic touches of his own. So, it was not heartbreaking for him to leave Disney to work in comic books.

On July 25, 1941, Kelly returned to the Disney studio to meet with Walt Disney to see if Disney could help him find cartoon work back east. Walt wrote three letters to various people describing Kelly as a "former employee" who had "a complete understanding of the handling of any and all of our characters" and urged them to get in touch with Kelly for work.

It was because of those letters that Kelly began to get freelance work with Lebeck at Western in New York. Kelly drew the comic books at his home in Bridgeport, Connecticut, and commuted to New York three days a week to deliver his finished work.

He ended up adapting the Disney features *The Three Caballeros* (in *Dell Four Color* #71 1945) and *Pinocchio* (in *Dell Four Color* # 92 1946) to comic books and provided some covers and advertisements for *Walt Disney's Comics and Stories*.

Kelly wrote to Walt Disney on May 25, 1960:

> Just in case I ever forgot to thank you, I'd like you to know that I, for one, have long appreciated the sort of training and atmosphere that you set up back there in the thirties. It was an astounding experiment

and experience as I look back on it. Certainly, it was the only education I ever received and hope I'm living up to a few of your hopes for other people.

However, Kelly's most significant Disney related work at Western/Dell was a series of two-page pantomime comic book stories featuring the gremlins.

In fact, his style was so distinctive and appealing that even though he was following the model sheets prepared by the Disney studio, over the years he has been falsely credited with creating the designs and supplying artwork for other projects featuring the Gremlins, including the pamphlet *Winter Draws On* that does not include any artwork by him but was drawn by Bill Justice.

In issue number four of the *Dell War Heroes* comic book (April 1943), there was a six-page story adapting the basic Roald Dahl tale done in a realistic style by an unknown writer and artist.

During the Battle of Britain, a young pilot named Gus is attacked by Gremlin Gus boring holes in his wing and engine cowling. His fellow pilots don't believe his story until Gremlin Gus pops up and spills a beer mug into the lap of one of them.

One day, Gus has to parachute out of his plane and grabs Gremlin Gus as he plummets and gets the little creature to tell his story. The new factories and air bases inadvertently destroyed the homes of the gremlins.

Gus explains that the "iron birds" are protecting homes, including the ones of the gremlins who will get their land back after the war.

Gremlin Gus convinces the other gremlins to now help the RAF pilots by doing things like plugging tank leaks and scrapping ice off wings. More important, they help pilot Gus to pass his medical exam so he can return to flying, which he does. The story ends with:

> And he was only one of hundreds who came to understand, love and respect these little people! He is, indeed, an unhappy man who goes up into the sky to fight saying, "I do not believe in gremlins!"

In *Walt Disney Comics and Stories* #33 (June 1943) there was a two-page story credited to animator (Fleischer, Warner Brothers, Lantz, Hanna-Barbera) and funny animal comic-book artist Vivie Risto. Risto was the son of Finnish immigrants and his real name was Oscar Wilho Risto. He had just begun doing comic book stories for Dell in 1942 after leaving Warner Bros.

When a new group of pilots arrive at an RAF air base, they discount the story of gremlins as "that fairy story." The enraged gremlins disable one of the planes during a fight with a squadron of Messerschmitts. Hours later, the pilot tries to convince his friends that it was the work of gremlins.

An unbelieving pilot is leaning back in his chair saying "Gremlins, bosh! Don't try to pull that kid story on me!" when one of the gremlins saws the back chair leg. The chair collapses and the pilot now on the floor moans, "O-w-w! Who did that?" and finds himself facing three little creatures who say in unison, "Gremlins!"

The Kelly stories that appeared in *Walt Disney's Comics And Stories* were written and drawn by him. They were each two pages with four rows. They were all "pantomime" strips, meaning that they contain no captions or dialog balloons and that the story is conveyed purely through action.

In a way, it is odd that Kelly did these stories because most of the stories and artwork for *Walt Disney's Comics and Stories* were produced by the office in Los Angeles and Kelly was in New York. However, Lebeck considered Kelly his star artist and liked that Kelly could draw cute characters and had an understanding of visual slapstick, two important aspects for the series.

WDCS #34 (July 1943)

Gremlin Gus struts across the airfield followed by two widgets struggling to carry a heavy tool box. Gus turns to see the widgets have disappeared and the box is left on the ground. Picking it up himself, he struggles to carry the unexpectedly heavy box to the wheel of a plane. When he opens the box to get his tools, inside are the two sheepish widgets.

Gus chases them away with his foot as he takes a drill bit to the wheel of an airplane. The curious widgets play with a nearby oil can and splash Gus, whose drill pops the tire. The exploding air sends Gus high in the air and he knocks the two widgets into the can. A whistling Gus walks proudly home followed by the two sad oil-covered widgets.

The final panel is a paper doll of Gremlin Gus done by Kelly.

WDCS # 35 (August 1943)

Two widgets start to saw away at the legs of a wooden chair when Gremlin Gus points them to move away. He flexes a saw and proceeds to cut away at all four legs so that it is balanced precariously. As a pilot with a newspaper approaches to sit in the wobbly chair, Gus and the widgets hide behind a spittoon to observe the fun as the chair collapses underneath the man when he finally sits.

Gremlin Gus proudly congratulates the widgets who take the saw to Gus' home and saw the wooden steps to the front door and the wooden chair so that Gus collapses when he uses them. The last panel in the story is Gus throwing the saw after the widgets fleeing into the night.

The final panel is a cut-out paper doll of a fifinella by Kelly.

WDCS #36 (September 1943)

Gremlin Gus lugs a round black bomb to the wheel of a plane. He carries a large wooden matchstick to light it. Two widgets riding on a grasshopper arrive and the insect bucks them off into Gus. He puts the two widgets over his knee and spanks them with the matchstick.

The two widgets climb into the open cockpit of the plane and start the engine. The wind from the propeller knocks over Gus and blows his derby hat down the field. The two widgets shake hands to congratulate themselves as Gus' hat blows into the top of a gasoline can on its side. Gus peers inside, but because it is so dark he can't see, so he lights the match to retrieve his hat and the can blows up.

The final panel has a burnt and shaken Gus wearing an El Ropo cigar band because his clothes have been blown off, while the two widgets follow behind staring innocently at the sky.

WDCS #37 (October 1943)

Gremlin Gus sets a ladder against the wheel of a plane and starts to climb up. Behind him, a mouse pops out of a hole in the ground and pulls the ladder down its hole causing Gus to fall on his face.

Two widgets standing nearby break out into laughter. An irritated Gus puts both of them over his knee and spanks them. The angry widgets get a round domed metal mousetrap with a piece of cheese to catch the mouse. Gus sees the trap and is curious. As he bends down to look at the cheese, the smiling mouse pops up out of his hole and pushes Gus into the trap and grabs the cheese to munch.

Gus, still trapped in the cage, turns it over to chase after the two widgets.

WDCS #38 (November 1943)

While the pilots are eating at the mess hall table, Gremlin Gus and two widgets use a string to climb up to the top of the table and overturn a pepper shaker, causing the pilots to sneeze uncontrollably.

The two widgets decide to help by blowing on the spilt pepper, but unfortunately, Gremlin Gus sneezes so hard that he is propelled backwards into a bottle of ketchup. An unsuspecting officer who is reading the paper picks up the bottle and empties it on his plate.

As he stabs his fork into his meal, he is surprised to find Gremlin Gus on the tip of his fork desperately pleading not to be eaten. The final panel has the officer falling over backward in his chair while Gus chases off the two widgets with the fork.

WDCS #39 (December 1943)

A tired Gremlin Gus yawns and stretches by an ashtray with a pipe. He decides to take a nap inside the comfy pipe. An unsuspecting officer picks up the pipe and pours tobacco into it. The tobacco suddenly flies out.

The determined pilot tamps down the tobacco into the pipe and his finger is bitten by Gus. The irritated officer looks into the pipe and Gus throws tobacco into his eye, forcing the officer to throw the pipe to the floor. Turning the pipe upside down, Gus runs away while the officer falls to the floor in tears.

WDCS #40 (January 1944)

Two pilots are playing ping pong on a table when the ball goes astray onto the floor. Gremlin Gus watching from behind a spittoon grabs the ball, but then one of the pilots picks it up with Gus hanging on precariously.

The pilot serves the ball and Gus opens his parachute as it flies through the air. This slows the flight of the ball, making it difficult for the other pilot to hit it back, but not impossible. Directly over the net, Gus tosses the ball high in the air and the two pilots end up hitting each other on the top of their heads, knocking each other out.

The last panel has them both laying across the table as a whistling Gus casually walks away.

WDCS #41 (February 1944)

A mess sergeant points to two men to start peeling a pile of potatoes on the table. Gremlin Gus uses the knife on the table as a catapult to send him and a potato flying at the back of the head of the sergeant. The angry man turns, assuming one of the two pilots threw it at him.

One of them points out Gus sitting on the sergeant's shoulder and grabs a pot to smash the gremlin. However, Gus slides down and the pot ends up on the sergeant's head. He stumbles outside and bumps into a general, knocking him down. The fallen general sees Gus on top of the pot and pulls out a gun to shoot him just as the sergeant pulls off the pot and sees the gun pointing at his face. He pleads with the angry general.

Inside, the two pilots grab two pies to throw at Gus, but they end up hitting the general and the sergeant on the top of their heads. The last panel is Gus casually walking away as he eats a piece of pie.

A one-page illustration of Gremlin Gus adapted from Walt Kelly's comic book work in *Walt Disney Comics and Stories* pops up mysteriously in *The Walt Disney Paint Book*, a coloring book from Whitman published in 1944.

It is the only gremlin drawing in the book which is otherwise filled with drawings of Mickey, Donald, and others, obviously adapted as well from comic-book panels.

Also prepared at the same time (but not drawn by Kelly) was a large one-panel, four-image cartoon produced for King Features Syndicate (who were distributing Disney comic strips) in 1943 that summarized the basic story of the Gremlins to be run in newspapers. The artwork was very similar in style to the *Dell War Heroes* comic book.

- *Image One.* Gremlins sitting forlornly on a tree stump watching planes in the air. "These are the Gremlins…a sad group of little people… sad because an army of men has invaded their woodland paradise, destroying their trees and flowers and erecting huge ugly buildings that hatched big noisy birds of war."

- *Image Two.* "But the Gremlins are peaceful no longer…under the leadership of Gremlin Gus they've decided that these ungainly birds of steel shall pay dearly for the havoc they have wrought!" Standing on a tree stump surrounded by saws, hammers, drills, axes, shovels, and other tools of destruction, a gremlin shouts to his brethren: "'Op to it, Gremlins! Get Busy! We'll never rest until we've had our revenge on these flying monsters! Stow away on every one of 'em! Bring down all you can…and plague the humans who fly 'em!"

- *Image Three.* Multiple gremlins attacking a British Spitfire in flight. "Equipped with their suction boots, they can stick to a plane in combat traveling at any speed. Sawing through wings, drilling bullet holes, and cutting gas lines, they work day and night to clear the skies of their mechanical enemies!"

- *Image Four.* A pilot in a parachute in the sky with a gremlin on a parachute next to him saying, "An' this is just the beginnin', Guv'nor…. You ain't seen nothin' yet!"

IDW Publishing released *Donald Duck* #18 (whole number 385) in October 2016. It featured a reprint of a thirty-six-page story entitled "Rue Brittania!" written by Lars Jensen and drawn by Flemming Andersen which first appeared in the Disney Swedish comic book *Kaelle Ankas Pocket* #330 (2006).

The story concerns "paranormalists" Donald Duck and his partner Fethry Duck who work for TNT (Tamers of Nonhuman Threats) trying to get rid of the gremlins plaguing an airfield.

The two ducks are sent to Big Missington Air Field in England, located just below Putney Swope to investigate some mysterious lights. When they arrive, they see the bright lights and are magically transported back in time to the airfield in the 1940s.

Donald is mistaken for the new flight instructor and Fethry as his engineer. They meet Wilkins, the commanding officer, and a flight instructor named Buzz Canyon. Canyon warns the two ducks that they are being troubled by gremlins, but Wilkins vehemently denies the existence of the creatures.

When Canyon take Donald and Fethry up into the air in a Tiger Moth bi-plane about to be sent to the salvage yard, they run into a gremlin who saws off the left wing. The trio parachutes to safety as the plane crashes into the sea.

Donald discovers that the nearby town of Putney Swope is infected with gremlin mania. The townspeople are baking gremlin biscuits, selling gremlin dolls, and singing and dancing to gremlin music, among other things. Even though he has seen one, Donald decides the best way to fight gremlins is to refuse to believe in them, hoping the creatures will be demoralized and leave.

However, Donald's vocal protests about the existence of gremlins results in them putting a porcupine in his shower, dumping a tree load of apples on his jeep, and other antics.

Donald and Fethry overhear Gremlin Gus telling his fellow gremlins that they must continue to fight because they have been forced to live underground due to their forest home having been cut down to build the airfield and they are now deafened by the drone of the planes.

While all the new pilots are out on flight training, Donald, Fethry, Wilkins, and Canyon are knocked off their feet by the rumbling of the earth. The gremlins run toward them and claim that they were conjuring something out of a great magic book to scare them all away, but inadvertently contacted an evil entity instead.

The sky starts raining frogs. They take off in a plane to assess the situation. Pilot Canyon gets knocked out, so Donald has to take over just in time to see in the sky an outline of a demonic head. Donald has to convince Wilkins to believe in gremlins because only when people believe in them can their magic work.

Wilkins does see them and the gremlins dissolve the huge head. It later turns out it was a gremlin trick where the gremlins had crows fly in formation to make the demon head and had made arrangements with the frogs to have the crows drop them out of the sky.

The magic book only made the bad weather. Now that the gremlins have convinced all the airfield personnel that they exist, they use the magic book to send Donald and Fethry back home to the 21st century where they find that the airfield has been abandoned for years.

An old gentleman in a coat and hat that obscures his face tells the duo that once Wilkins started believing in gremlins, he lobbied his superiors to shut the place down. Donald decides to tell his superiors that after investigating the mysterious lights, he decided it was just a natural phenomenon and not something supernatural.

The story ends with the old man talking with the gremlins, who have not aged a day. They had determined that they needed to attract some "monster hunters" with an open mind to be able to convince Wilkins.

It turns out that the old man is actually a much aged Wilkins who is happy to now admit "I do believe in Gremlins" as the rainy weather clears and in the distance is a rainbow.

In addition, the cover is a reprint of the cover done by Walt Kelly for Dell's *Walt Disney's Comics and Stories* Vol. 3 No. 10 (July 1943) featuring Donald Duck in an airplane trying to swat away Gremlin Gus and his friends with a flyswatter as they attack Donald's little red plane.

The story echoes the premise of the original Dahl story that happy is the man who admits to believing in Gremlins because otherwise disasters would happen.

CHAPTER FIFTEEN

Gremlin Insignia

Another way in which Disney encouraged people to think of *Disney* gremlins when they thought of gremlins was to use the creatures on military insignias.

The tradition of military insignias goes back to the Middle Ages when knights used a distinctive heraldry crest on the breastplate of their armor or on their shields to identify themselves to other knights.

One of the earliest animated cartoon character insignias that was still in use in World War II was done by animator Walter Lantz of Oswald the Rabbit for the U.S. Navy's Observation Squadron in 1930.

During World War II, the Disney studio received hundreds of requests for insignia designs from various branches of the U.S. armed services and civilian support organizations. Walt even honored requests for insignias from military units serving with Allied countries, including Canada, France, Poland, New Zealand, South Africa, and of course, Britain.

Walt complied without hesitation and ended up supplying approximately 1,200 emblems at no cost. Walt felt it was his duty, and later told author Bob Thomas:

> How could you turn them down? They meant a lot to the men who were fighting and they didn't know who else to go to. I had to do it. Those kids grew up on Mickey Mouse. I owed it to them.

Roy Disney estimated that it cost the studio about twenty-five dollars for each insignia to cover time, labor, and materials.

The famous Flying Tiger design for the American Volunteer Group under the command of Captain Claire Chennault was done by Disney artist Hank Porter from a design by Roy Williams.

Most insignias featured Donald Duck, whose feisty personality seemed to align well with the needs of most groups. Mickey Mouse was not warlike in nature and appeared on very few designs and usually ended up on those for home-front activities.

After the requested emblems were created, they were sent to the War Department for approval. Only a small handful were rejected, and even these were accepted after slight modifications. One of the rules was no use of numbers of any kind, so Disney came up with a workaround using stars in place of numbers so, for instance, five stars at top and six at bottom translated into the "56th."

Some of those designs still exist today, even if the units themselves were long since disbanded after the war, on such things as vintage Christmas cards, mugs, buttons, decals, and inside comic books.

Two different series of matchbook covers with the Disney insignias were produced for the National Match Company and there was a series of gummed and perforated poster stamps of the insignia images to be affixed inside five booklets designed like regular stamp albums. Each booklet held 50 stamps.

Hank Porter was assigned to supervise a unit of artists doing insignia work. The group included Roy Williams, Van Kaufman, George Goepper, Ed Parks, and Bill Justice. However, it was Porter who did most of the designs. His versatility and talent were in demand for many specialty Disney projects.

Members of the various branches of the armed forces had seen all the marketing images of Disney's gremlins and were intrigued. In fact, despite not appearing in any animated film, the gremlins were among the top five requested Disney characters.

The studio produced over twenty-eight insignias featuring the Disney gremlins, including ones for the 12th Combat Camera Unit Detachment, 546th Bombardment Squadron, the 17th Weather Squadron, the Royal Canadian Air Force, and the Royal Netherland Military Flying School.

It has been assumed that Bill Justice did many if not all of these designs because of his connection with *The Gremlins*, although Porter obviously did some as well.

The fifinella insignia has been discussed at length in chapter four. A Disney gremlin insignia done for the state of Minnesota lasted over half a century, while other Gremlin insignias vanished after the war when their units were shut down.

Thanks to the research work of Lt. Colonel Thomas J O'Connor and Major Andrew "Ace" Browning, the story of a significant Gremlin patch has been documented.

Shortly after the Civil Air Patrol (CAP) came under control and direction of the Army, the Minnesota Wing submitted a request to Disney for permission to use one of their gremlins in an emblem.

CAP was seen as a way to use America's civilian aviation resources to aid the war effort instead of simply grounding them. The organization assumed many missions, including anti-submarine patrol and warfare, border patrols, towing targets for aerial gunnery practice, search-and-rescue operations, and courier services.

Major Horace E Read, Minnesota's 71st wing commander, announced on March 31, 1943, in the *St. Cloud Daily Times* that the Disney studio had agreed to get behind Minnesota Wing's request and design an emblem featuring a gremlin. It is probable that Bill Justice designed Minnesota Wing's shoulder patch.

The insignia had a completely brown-suited gremlin riding on a winged circle which had a white triangle with three red propeller wings in the center. That blue disc with the interior triangle was the first national insignia for the Civil Air Patrol beginning February 1942. This state insignia used the already approved national insignia as its core.

By 1944, members in the wing had already started making their own unofficial gremlin patches based on the Disney design and wearing them on the right shoulder of their flight suits with the national patch still being worn on the left.

Some hand-painted leather and canvas flight jacket patches featuring the artwork were also made. Minnesota Wing's gremlin patch was finally approved by National Headquarters for wear on April 4, 1950, which had not previously approved any individual state patches until 1948.

Over the decades, the original design started to morph dramatically and bore only slight resemblance to the original design. The expressive eyes had become just large dots and the gloves disappeared, among other variations.

During the mid-1990s, the wing started to use the original Disney character design in various ways, most notably in the monthly *Wing-Tips* newsletter, volleyball T-shirts, annual ski trip bandanas, and the 1999–2002 cadet encampment patch.

In 1997, Captain Andrew Browning of Farmington Composite Squadron had 200 special-edition collector wing patches manufactured using the gremlin as it was originally intended. Then, nearly fifty-eight years after Walt Disney approved use of his gremlin character, Colonel Dale E Hoium, Minnesota wing commander, approved a new and accurate patch design for wear on April 14, 2001.

The previous half-century old patch was officially retired from use on December 31, 2001.

CHAPTER SIXTEEN

The Animated Feature

Dahl's original short story was too slight to be a feature film since it simply introduced the gremlins and then had them change their ways and help an injured pilot get back into the air. It was more of a short vignette than a fleshed-out, full-sized story.

However, Walt saw that this basic concept and the characters had possibilities and could be easily expanded. Two full-length treatments were prepared for the proposed feature.

The first treatment is 155 pages long and is dated May 18, 1943. It was dedicated to the fighter pilots of the RAF who turned "mortal danger into immortal fantasy. They gave the gremlins birth—and the echo of their laughter with which they greeted their creation, grew into a wind that blew across the world to confound all tyrants!"

The film would have begun with a tranquil British countryside that transforms into a war-torn landscape to indicate how the idyllic home of the gremlins (and the British) had been shattered by the hostilities.

German bombers are flying toward the coast to do more damage and a squadron of Spitfire planes are sent up to engage them. One Spitfire crash lands near a farm. Looking at the damage, the tall red-headed young pilot, Scotty, remarks, "Those aren't bullet holes. That's the work of Gremlins."

The scene shifts to the western desert of North Africa (where Dahl had actually crashed his plane) to show other damaged planes while the narrator explains gremlins and that they can only be seen by combat pilots.

The point of view shifts to the cockpit of a fighter pilot so that the audience can see the gremlins. Once in the air, escorting a bomber plane, the Spitfire is attacked, with the enemy tracer bullets turning into gremlins drilling holes into the plane. The plane crashes.

At Gremlin Headquarters, located between walls and below buildings at the fictional Dartford Hill Fighter Station, the narrator explains fifinellas and widgets. Gremlin Gus is the leader of the gremlins and the teacher of young widgets.

This scene also introduces a Goofy gremlin (who later comically runs away from a rolling pool ball under a pool table) and a Dopey gremlin similar to comedian Harpo Marx, to make gremlins seem a bit more comical and likeable rather than deadly.

Gremlin Gus lectures them all that this is war and that they need to do damage that is not so easily repaired. While looking through a newspaper, he scoffs at gremlins being blamed for non-aircraft related mischief, sees an artist's interpretation of a gremlin that he finds personally insulting, and discovers there is one pilot, Rip Wilson, who seems to have remained untouched from gremlin troubles.

The gremlins then chant the story of why they do such harm. They were driven out of their peaceful woodland home when it was cut down and destroyed to make room for hangars and airplanes. They have sworn revenge against "these metal creatures and those who fly them" by causing whatever harm they can.

Rip Wilson (who the draft describes as looking like a younger Fred Astaire) is part of a squadron composed of Scotty and another pilot named Deacon Smith.

When they land, Sgt. Yorky comments that Rip's plane has not been bothered by gremlins. Rip doesn't believe in such nonsense and firmly says so, causing nearby invisible gremlins to get riled up. Yorky shows Rip that he has built a trap to catch gremlins with used postage stamps as bait.

Another air battle sequence is shown, with many pilots eliminated. Scotty holds up a bandaged hand claiming it was the result of an encounter with spandules. The spandules are shown to be less civilized than regular gremlins in a scene depicting them icing up the wing of a Spitfire.

Rip remains unconvinced, but the gremlins are listening to his unflattering comments about them.

The film then shifts to widget school where the young creatures dutifully write out "We hate planes" and break up airplane toys. However, the widgets also enjoy doing mischief to the older gremlins simply because it is their nature. Gremlin Gus is supervising all of this activity and when he hears of Rip's remarks, he decides to take action.

He has fifinellas tempt spandules down near the ground where they breathe their icy vapor into Rip's room, causing him to catch a bad cold. The next morning when Rip takes to the air, he is light-headed and sneezing. He confronts a German plane and since he is not paying attention, his plane is hit.

Surprisingly, he comes face-to-face with Gremlin Gus in the cockpit who, along with other gremlins, tear apart Rip's plane. Gremlin Gus explains that it is only the plane they are after and assists the woozy Rip to bail out and parachute to safety into the English Channel.

In Berlin, Hitler is ranting about the English papers giving credit to gremlins rather than Nazis for downed British aircraft.

Rip, in a hospital recuperating, listens to Hitler's speech. Gremlin Gus appears to Rip and tells him about the destruction of their homes. Rip tries to explain that the destruction wasn't intentional and that they were unaware that anybody lived there. He also emphasized that the air bases had to be built to defend their homes and the Gremlins' homes as well. He says:

> We're defending you from the most savage gangsters the world's ever dealt with—the Nazis—and these airplanes are the best weapons for that job. We're fighting so that people can say, hear and believe anything they want to...believe in fairies if they like...believe in you, for instance. You represent imagination. That's one thing the "New Order" can't stand.

The radio is still on and Gremlin Gus hears Hitler's increasing insults about Gremlins and is converted to helping win the war against the Nazis.

The final scene is the big Battle of Britain. Scotty is a casualty, but the Gremlins have joined in to the fight, riding tracer bullets to the Nazi planes where they aggressively go about their mayhem. The final shot is Hitler blaming the gremlins for the defeat.

Over forty-five different people looked over this draft and submitted suggestions. Dahl was not sent a copy. The draft featured the sequence that would have had Hitler "sputtering a flood of unintelligible German" nonsense as he complains to his top staff members Goebbels and Goering that British newspapers have been giving credit to gremlins for all the wonderful efforts undertaken by Hitler's air force, the Luftwaffe.

The session would have been interrupted by Mussolini entering "looking pretty battered and holding his hands up sort of like an Italian chef describing a dish of spaghetti." This particular sequence disturbed Disney's legal counsel Gunther Lessing who effectively lobbied for its removal with comments like "pure propaganda stuff which should not be indulged in here."

Lessing's memo to Roy Disney dated June 1, 1943, read:

> I read the script of *Gremlins of the RAF* over the weekend. In my opinion, the story up to the time Rip is shot down has great possibilities. There is fine opportunity to develop cartoon personalities, humor and suspense. However, from then on, the story looks as if it were written in a hurry or by a different person from the one who started it.
>
> I do not like what happens while Rip is falling from his plane. We did something like it in *Dumbo* (1941). It makes things drag and does not create the suspense which evidently is desired. Furthermore, it is contrary to what should be the nature of the Gremlins. It is a bit artificial to have them antagonistic to planes and not to the flyer.

Then the interludes with Hitler are in the nature of short story technique and has no place in a feature. Furthermore it is pure propaganda stuff which should not be indulged in here.

Then Rip's convincing of Gus Gremlin is not the best treatment. Why not carry on the idea of Yorky's invention of a trap to catch Gremlins? Why not let Yorky catch Gus and over a mug of beer (like in a former script) have a scene with Yorky and Gus getting a little tipsy and arguing it out.

I also like the idea, if it can be done, with trick photography of the Gremlins helping Rip stand his physical examination. This could be simplified but in the end can probably create suspense and a lot of action.

Then again, the little love theme with the nurse and war worker which was in the former script, should help the story. I assume that they intend to use process photography with live action and cartoon. A handsome leading man and a good looking girl should help the picture. Yorky seems to be a good character and a lot could be done with him.

There are a lot of discrepancies such as the fact that the Spandules dissolving when they hit below the stratosphere and still come down to Rip's window and blow their breath into his room. Of course, such things can be smoothed out.

Over three dozen other opinions were expressed about this draft, but achieving no real consensus for the direction of the story other than this one just didn't seem to work.

In a May 1943 story conference on another project, Walt let slip a plan he had in the back of his mind to tie the gremlins story together:

Let's make a study of what technique we can develop for music under narration. When we get into long length things we go like hell.

In a feature we've got to find places where it doesn't go that fast—to give relief. Otherwise it's pound, pound, pound. Narration technique is in. Especially in foreign versions. On Gremlins, I'm using a narrator—in a few words he can bridge a gap.

The second full-length treatment is dated June 9, 1943, but is closer in length to about one hundred pages in an attempt to better focus the slight story. The addition of large chunks of narration, a suggestion from Walt, is now evident, as well as a dose of patriotic exhortation concerning the need to join together to fight a single enemy.

When Gremlin Gus is accused of fraternizing with a human by a court of gremlins and pleads that it is good to help the pilots and their planes defeat the Nazis, an unexploded German bomb crashes into the middle of the gathering as proof. Basically, the treatment tries to veer away from

Gremlins' destruction of RAF aircraft. It concentrates more on the origin of the gremlins and their society and why they are being destructive. The material that featured Hitler is gone entirely.

A note sent to Walt with the treatment states:

> At first we considered following parts of the book, but decided that, while the book's continuity and climax is okay for reading, it really doesn't hold together as a picture.

> We also felt that the present outline gives better opportunity for more varied characterization and gagging on the Gremlins. In view of the shortened footage, we have indicated no spot for an outstanding song number; but it is possible that a Gremlin School song could be built up in that sequence.

Another story version that was pitched but rejected was the Gremlins having to defeat their own little version of Hitler before aiding the Allies in battling the real thing.

Walt wrote to Dahl on March 19, 1943:

> Dear Stalky;

> We have abandoned our plans to make the GREMLINS a combination of live action and cartoon, and instead have decided to make it one hundred percent cartoon, with the story being told from the GREMLIN's angle.

> We are now working along this line and it is shaping up rather fast, but we do get stuck on a lot of the GREMLIN business. A Gremlinologist of your caliber would come in most handy right now. What do you think are the chances of the Embassy letting you get away and coming out here for a while.

> It would help us very much. We would be willing to make any arrangements in the way of expenses for your stay while here, so I wonder if you would go into the matter and let us know if there is any possibility of your spending some time with us.

> At this point there are several important things upon which you could assist us, and we don't want to go too far with our present treatment and then find it was not in good taste from the GREMLIN's angle.

> I would like to lay my plans to put this picture in work within a few months, which would enable us to get it out approximately the first of next year, so you see, any help you could give us right now would be very beneficial. If you can get away, please let me know when, and what procedure we should follow to effect your trip out here.

> Kindest regards, Walt.

Dahl wrote to Jim Bodrero the first week of June 1943:

> I do hope that Walt will not reconsider the idea of making a composite film. You cannot imagine the relief and joy which Air Ministry expressed when we told them some time ago that he had finally decided to make it a pure cartoon.
>
> Heaven forbid that I should try to teach him his business, but because of this I am quite certain that if we are going to have actual photographs of actual people and actual aeroplanes in this film, there is going to be trouble and strife before we have gone very far.

There was no consensus of what to call the finished film. The storymen couldn't seem to find the right hook for the story, but a story title needed to be officially registered to protect the project from competing studios.

A memo from October 22, 1942, shows that the following titles suggested by Jim Bodereo were registered with the Hays Office: *Gay Gremlins, Gremlin Lore, Gremlin Gambols, Gremlins in the Sky, We've Got Gremlins, Gremlin Trouble, Widgets Next in Wings, The Helpful Gremlins, The Gremlin Legend, We Fly With Gremlins, Hi-Flying Gremlins,* and *Look! Gremlins!*

Don Niles sent a memo to Walt indicating that he was concerned that none of the titles included the names "fifinella" or "spandule," but that "the Hays office rules permit us to register only 13 more features and 8 more shorts titles".

There is no indication that the film was referred to by any title other than *The Gremlins* or *Gremlins of the RAF* in any official documents or even memos. More often, it was just simply referred to as *Gremlins*.

Finally, on December 18, 1943, Walt wrote to Dahl:

> Definitely the Gremlins will not be made as a feature because of the feeling on the distributor's part that the public has become tired of so many war films.
>
> We have given considerable thought to the possibility of making the Gremlins into a short and I have personally endeavored to generate some interest among the various crews, but haven't met with any degree of success.
>
> However, if we ever hit upon an angle that seems right for production, we'll get in touch with you.

That proposed short had actually been put together on storyboards in August 1943 and ultimately rejected. It was necessary to cram in lots of information to introduce the characters, so it lacked the lightheartedness of typical Disney entertainment shorts.

The gremlins no longer lived in the woodlands, but were now inhabitants of the "fleecy cloud banks that reach up into the stratosphere beyond the sight of man." They have lived there since the beginning of time in eternal peace. On the storyboards, perhaps taking an artistic cue from the "Pastoral Symphony" segment of *Fantasia* (1940), their swirling cloud castles were in pastel shades of blue and pink.

At first, they were amused by man's attempts to fly, but once war came, the quaint man-made metal devices became deadly weapons of destruction, leaving "devastation and confusion" in their wake as they invaded the realm of the gremlins and tore through the cloud kingdom.

All the gremlins swore an oath to get rid of these "monsters of metal who have destroyed our peace and happiness" and never cease making life miserable for those who flew them until the last one was driven from the skies.

After this explanatory material, the scene shifts to an airfield where a Wellington aircraft is making an emergency crash landing, causing damage to the runaway. An intelligence officer does a debriefing of the crew who claim that it was "just a bit of Gremlin trouble."

The scene dissolves to the cloud kingdom of the gremlins where Gremlin Gus is doing his own debrief. Apparently, the plane plowed through a thick cloud bank and a "St. Elmo's Fire"-type Gremlin looking like a jagged lightning bolt gets into the interior and causes a variety of havoc.

These gremlins were just the warm-up and they turn over the attack to the more familiar flight-suited gremlins. The plane flies low several miles below Rotterdam, following the river and trying to be as inconspicuous as possible.

Unfortunately, the gremlins had gotten into the flares, set the interior on fire, and lit up the sky so that the enemy could easily see the plane and fill the air with flak. The plane manages to make its way to the mission at Felshaven and despite some interference from gremlins, drops its bombs and blows up the bridge spanning the river.

On their way home, the plane runs into some thick bad weather. A gremlin whispers in the ear of the pilot, convincing him to take a chance and fly right through it rather than going around it. The gremlins do several tricks to prevent the plane from getting out of the dangerous poor visiblity but eventually, the pilot rises above the clouds.

Then the haughty spandules take over, icing the wings and the propeller so the plane begins to plummet. The crew prepares to bail out with Tail Gunner Yorky to jump first when they reach 10,000 feet. But as Yorky stands over the open bomb-bay door, the spandules abandon the ship because they can't stand the lower altitudes.

As the windshield clears, the ice flies off the propeller, and the controls begin to respond again, a radio order is shouted to a startled Yorky not to jump. Of course, Yorky falls out the open hatch and there is a series of complicated physical gags as he tries, and eventually succeeds, in getting back inside.

A lone German fighter attacks the plane and the surprised crew finds that the gremlins play no favorites as they go after the easier target. There follows a series of wordless gags as the gremlins tear apart the German fighter, much to the consternation of its pilot.

The British bomber makes it back to the shores of England, but the pea soup fog requires a blind landing that was depicted at the beginning of the cartoon.

The intelligence officer states:

> Very interesting, Gentlemen. But...ah...this Gremlin thing looks jolly bad on a flight report...might suggest following the rules a little closer...no need to call on imaginary characters to excuse your own errors in...ah...judgment. However, must say the job was well done...."

The cartoon then dissolves back to the clouds where Gremlin Gus says:

> Well done, lads...nice work. If we can keep this up it won't be long before our skies are clear of these destructive and obnoxious monsters. These....

Gus is interrupted by a huge plane zooming through the homes of the gremlins. Gus points at the offending intruder plane and shouts:

> After 'em, Lads! Carry on! It may take time, but we'll never let up! It's either Gremlins or airplanes—and Gremlins Goes on Forever!!

After the rejection of that entertainment short, Ham Luske suggested that the project might be formatted into a training film to help prevent pilot carelessness, using the material already developed:

> I honestly think there is something to the idea of making it into a training film. We might get a contract with an awful lot of the work already done on it.

An interesting oddity is a training film with a title card stating *Fundamental Fixed Gunnery Approaches*. It was copyrighted 1943 and produced under the supervision of the Bureau of Aeronautics by Walt Disney Productions with technical direction by the Naval Air Operational Training Command.

Most of Disney's training films made for the branches of the armed forces during World War II are undocumented, with the government taking all materials connected with the making of the films as well as the films themselves once they were completed, so if it is difficult to tell whether this film featured gremlins, but an interesting image surfaced fairly recently.

One point in the film shows five squat cartoony male creatures, each wearing a black varsity sweatshirt with a big "G" on the chest, using wires to pull on the airplane's wings to tilt it on its side during a mission. They wear goggles and pilot helmets. The assumption is that the flying men are gremlins, but they bear no similarity to the official Disney design.

Some have argued that these are not gremlins, but animated representations of gravity and G-force that cause the plane to bank so extremely. In addition, the appearance of only five might refer to 5 Gs of force. However, without access to the narration, it is difficult to make a definitive conclusion.

United Artists showed interest in distributing Disney's feature film about gremlins because they had released *Victory Through Air Power* (1943) when Walt's regular distributor RKO balked at doing so. Earlier, United Artists had released Disney short cartoons and Walt was personal friends with co-owners Mary Pickford and Charlie Chaplin.

Later, RKO would refuse to release the first True-Life Adventure film and Walt had to arrange to have it shown and win an Oscar before RKO buckled. Once RKO saw gremlin mania taking hold of the country, they relented about releasing a feature about Disney gremlins.

In addition to Disney sending out stills and press releases to publications and trade papers, RKO did as well.

Leon J. Bamberger, the sales promotion manager of RKO, sent Walt a short letter on June 8, 1943:

> Inasmuch as I believe you are making a picture concerning the Gremlins I thought you would like to see the enclosed article regarding how the Gremlins eat postage stamps.
>
> Since we have about ten million collectors of postage stamps in this country alone, any incident incorporated in the picture having to do with the Gremlins eating stamps I am sure would prove very interesting to this section of the public as well as audiences generally.

In November 1942, producer Cecil D. DeMille announced he was going to put a sequence with gremlins into a film he was currently working on. but later changed his mind or else the film never developed.

It has been speculated that DeMille may have been thinking of the sequence for the World War II "true story" feature film *The Story of Dr. Wassell* (1944) that he began work on around mid-1942.

Perhaps something that is still so appealing about the gremlins is that even after all these decades so many mysteries still swirl around the project.

CHAPTER SEVENTEEN

What Killed the Gremlins?

There is no one "smoking gun" for the death of the gremlins project. However, it is apparent that a combination of challenges contributed to its cancellation.

In his article "Walt Disney and *The Gremlins*: An Unfinished Story," animation historian John Cawley wrote that as quickly as the public had embraced gremlins, they had now tired of them just as quickly:

> By February [1943], it appeared that all the forces on Earth were fighting the completion of the film. Polls showed that filmgoers were tiring of war theme pictures. An Associated Press article titled "Gremlin Stuff is Getting Tiresome" echoed many media columnists when it stated that "They've been whimsied to pieces," and that "very soon any member of the general public who ventures to wax coy about them will run the risk of getting his itsy-bitsy block stoved in."

> In March, an aviation magazine editor also complained about the constant attention to Gremlins. The problem was not so much the overabundance of material, but the image they gave the RAF: "Surely, the greatest flying and fighting service is not going to ape Sir James Barrie at his worst."

By July, Walt told Dahl that instead of a feature, the Disney studio wanted to do the gremlins subject as a short cartoon and again expressed his concern over the infamous Clause 12 suggesting the British Air Ministry approval.

In a letter to Dahl dated July 2, Walt suggests:

> Because of its timely nature and the fact that it should be out now, everybody thinks we ought to put it out as a short.... The complications that arise with the R.A.F. are other reasons why we do not want to consider the feature angle.

> Every time I refer to Clause 12, I become a little apprehensive of what I may be facing. With the amount of money that is required to spend

on a feature of this type, we cannot be subjected to the whims of certain people, including yourself. I do not mean this unkindly or in any sense as a criticism, but we feel it is simply not good business to undertake the production of the Gremlins as a feature at this time with so much risk involved.

I might fly to Canada to look things over and whatever information seems pertinent I can pass on to the boys. I believe they can get a lot out of films—when you get too authentic on the Gremlins, I feel it handicaps the subject for cartoon entertainment.

Dahl had planned so that Walt and some of his staff could visit the Royal Canadian Air Force headquarters to obtain material for the film. He had made arrangements for Walt's crew to see Spitfires flying and an operational squadron of Hurricanes on the job with the pilots at readiness and in the dispersal huts in hopes of getting them all excited again about doing the feature. Walt never went.

A lengthy story conference on the project was held August 20, 1943, with Jim Bodrero, Ted Sears, Ham Luske, Wilfred Jackson, Dave Hand, Bill Berg, Dick Shaw, Bill Justice, Perce Pearce, Dick Kinney, and H.C. Holling in attendance trying to see if there was any way to go forward.

While Walt had already decided a month earlier that the material would be used to quickly produce a short, these men had put so much time and effort into the project that they decided to have one final meeting to see if there were any possibilities of still doing a feature.

Luske championed the approach of using live action combined with animation. He stated:

If you put [animated] fictitious pilots and fictitious Gremlins together, I don't get any punch out of it.

Wilfred Jackson brought up the concern of trying to animate a realistic human figure, even if only the hands and feet were shown or just a silhouette from the back. Even the use of rotoscoping (shooting live action as a reference and then tracing over it, perhaps with some artistic exaggeration) had resulted in very stiff figures that did not move naturally.

Perce Pearce remarked at the meeting:

Basically if these little guys are the pilots' alibis for their own stupidity, dereliction of duty, neglect, then you are taking some of the glamour off the RAF for me....

These Gremlins are very, very heavy villains to me.... They're cute little guys that are nasty, and the crew doesn't have a chance to pay them off. The fact that they're representing the German bullets is enough to tell me that they are the spirit of the enemy.

Others agreed that any attempt to try to create some sympathy for the gremlin mayhem just resulted in trying to get audiences to accept and perhaps cheer for damage to Allied planes and pilots.

While the pilots may have had a certain concept of the gremlins and how they helped alleviate some of the stress of combat and other challenges, communicating that same feeling to an audience completely unfamiliar with the pilots' culture was almost impossible.

Problems were discussed including how to make the film appealing and accessible to a general audience while still being authentic for professional airmen. The problems seemed insurmountable. After the meeting, the men gave their suggestions to Walt, and the picture was abandoned.

In September 1943, the charge number for *The Gremlins* was closed, meaning no more money could be spent on the project. Word was sent out to stop any work on *Gremlins* and to move on to other things.

Walt wrote to Dahl in early December 1943 that all plans for the film had been cancelled and that he had "personally endeavored to generate some interest among the various crews, but haven't met with any degree of success."

Over seven decades later, not one person believes that the real reason Walt cancelled the project was because he couldn't get his crews interested in it. There are countless stories of Walt inspiring his staff when confronted with a seemingly insurmountable challenge if Walt himself was convinced of the vision.

In reality, Walt had lost interest in producing any type of film project involving gremlins. He was tired of all the struggles he had to face, including dealing with Dahl who had proven much less cooperative than his initial charm had suggested.

The real mystery may be why Walt was so stubborn to keep pushing the project with all the mounting challenges. It is quite possible that he felt the need to produce something bigger since he had geared his studio to make feature films just before the war broke out.

In addition, he longed to do a project without military advisers constantly peering over his shoulder, nitpicking and challenging his decisions and needlessly delaying production.

Walt had gotten interested in aviation as evidenced by his commitment to the film *Victory Through Air Power* and using gremlins would have given him a chance to explore that subject with some creative freedom rather than be constrained by documentary material.

Animator Bill Justice claimed that there was legitimate concern among his fellow animators that by the time the feature would be finished the war would be over and the subject matter hopelessly out of date and quaint at best, not timeless like *Snow White*.

The over-saturation of the market with non-Disney gremlin stories and illustrations certainly did not bring confidence to Roy Disney and others that the Disney version would find an enthusiastic, receptive audience or a significant profit to offset the time and cost involved.

Animator Frank Thomas recalled that by the time he left for military service late in 1942, the staff at the Disney studio already considered the project dead. Years later when he and animator Ollie Johnston interviewed storyman T. Hee, who was intimately involved with the film for a book they were working on about animation, they discovered another possible explanation for its abandonment.

Hee remembered a meeting in Los Angeles with Walt, some Disney storymen (including Hee), several Disney animators, and a group of visiting RAF pilots. Apparently, to Walt's surprise, the pilots didn't truly believe in gremlins, but considered it all a "big joke" and Walt feared the public wouldn't believe in gremlins if the pilots didn't.

Of course, there is also the possibility that while RAF pilots believed in gremlins, they did not talk about them in a serious manner with the general public, for fear of ridicule.

Hee told interviewer Richard Hubler:

> This was during the war. I was ready to go home and started walking out toward the parking lot. Walt was behind me and caught up with me and said, "Where are you going?" I said, "I'm going home."
>
> He says, "I've got to go out here to see some R.A.F. flyers out in Bel Air, talk about the Gremlins. You want to go along?" I said, "Yeah, sounds good, but I'd better call my wife and tell her I'll be late." He said, "Okay."
>
> So I called my wife and said, "I'm going out with Walt to Bel Air and will probably eat out there somewhere so don't wait dinner for me."
>
> She said, "What time will you be home?" and I said, "I don't know." So, on the way down he talked all about this gremlin film, about these little guys that came out on the wings, saving the R.A.F. flyers and everything.
>
> We got down to this kind of a deep canyon and a big old house and it was colder and foggier than hell down there. The windows were open in every room, with windows from ceiling to floor, the doors were open. The R.A.F. men were all in their uniforms and the British women were in there with their low cut, sleeveless gowns and Walt and I had our overcoats on.
>
> We hesitated about taking them off because it was so God damned cold in there but they had fireplaces going in every room.

Finally we took them off and they served us drinks and these were the typical R.A.F. flyers—like the [actor] Terry Thomas guys—with the big moustaches, the whole thing, you know. They were talking in that very, very British, clipped way—very difficult to understand and the women were even more British.

Both of us being Midwesterners I think that that kind of grated on our ears, but most of the evening, before we had dinner, most of the R.A.F. flyers were in the den and they were telling off-color stories and Walt was laughing at them because they were funny.

But he wasn't there for that, he was there to talk about the gremlins for the film. Every time he'd bring it up, why they'd get off on some other tactic about their experiences. So we had dinner and I could see that Walt wasn't too happy because he couldn't get the conversation back to the gremlins.

We left late, pretty close to midnight, and we got in the car and he was silent and I said something about, "You know what you could do with those gremlins...." He said, "I'm not going to do the film." I said, "You're not?" And that was the end of it.

Supporters of this theory that Walt worried that even the RAF didn't take gremlins seriously enough point to Walt's caution in the making of the feature film *Darby O'Gill and The Little People* in 1959. The leprechaun stories of H.T. Kavanaugh had captured Walt's fancy even as early as the mid-1940s, but it wasn't until Walt himself was convinced that the Irish truly believed in the wee folk that he started to actively work on the film.

Certainly Walt's growing frustration with his studio enmeshed in the making of training films, not generating enough income, and having to deal with the whims of the military on production matters didn't help. In particular, the infamous Clause 12 connected with the gremlin project which allowed an outside entity to overrule Walt's decisions even at the very last minute was a deciding factor.

Dahl had his own theory about why the film was never made. In his 1977 autobiographical essay entitled "Lucky Break," he stated:

My Gremlin story was published as a children's book in New York and London, full of Disney's color illustrations, and it was called, of course, *The Gremlins*. Copies are very scarce now and hard to come by. I myself have only one. The film, also, was never finished.

I have a feeling that Disney was not really comfortable with this particular fantasy. Out there in Hollywood, he was a long way away from the Great War in the Air that was going on in Europe. Furthermore, it was a story about the Royal Air Force and not about his own countrymen, and that, I think, added to his sense of bewilderment. So in the end, he lost interest and dropped the whole idea.

Dahl emphasized this point in a 1984 interview with historian Robin Allan:

> [Walt] was totally American. My Gremlins book was European. He'd spent seven million dollars on it [Walt didn't, but this is typical Dahl exaggeration] and was going to go ahead and then an increasing number of R.A.F. pilots came out to California in 1943 to ferry airplanes back to England.
>
> He would call them in, and each one told him a different story about what Gremlins were and he got so befuddled by it, he didn't realize there was no such thing as authentic Gremlins' legend. I made it up. And he thought, "What do I do? Where do I go? Everyone's got a different story."
>
> And he cancelled the film just like that. It could have been successful.... [Walt] had no feeling for England in any way. Or Europe. It was too English, totally English. He was not into it. He was a hundred percent American. A hundred percent.

Certainly, Dahl's unavailability to the Disney studio as well as his constant criticisms about anything Disney was doing with the project were major factors in the film not being made. More and more, Walt sent Dahl's letters to Roy for a response, finding them to be increasingly bothersome and petty.

Dahl may have been superficially charming in person, but even a cursory glance at the correspondence from him to the Disney studio reveals an author who delayed development of the project, prevented opportunities for the project to evolve, and was demanding and arrogant. Many others have described Dahl as being "impossible" when working with others on a project.

In addition, as the project dragged on and no money would be coming his way but going to charity, Dahl got bored with it all and wanted to move on to something else.

It might even be assumed from the tone of the some of the correspondence that Dahl was using this project to position himself in a new career as an author. He was less interested in the story than the leverage it would give him for future, more important writing assignments.

The gremlins project made Dahl "bankable" as a writer and in 1943 he was taken on by literary agent Ann Watkins and went on to increased fame as an author.

His writing career included a novel, *Sometime Never* (1948), which took a much darker look at gremlins who short-circuited spark plugs of Spitfires by sitting on them ("It is a delightful sensation anyway.") and the gremlin dictator who bullies his subjects but also appeases them with snozzberries. The book was not embraced by the public and is little remembered today.

Another factor in the film not being made is that in an attempt to get an American audience familiar with gremlins, Walt had started the promotion for the film much too early and created an anticipation that waned when there was no clear date for the finished film. The artwork, the book, the insignias, the merchandise, the comic books, and the mentions in the newspaper columns had all geared up the audience's excitement, but there was nothing to satisfy their interest.

While *The Gremlins* was the only feature-length animated project shelved by Disney during World War II, other smaller films were also developed during this same time period and never completed.

These animated shorts included *Guerrilla Duck* with Donald Duck attempting to intercept a "Jap Troop Train" in Malaya and in *The Lone Raider* matching wits with a Japanese sentry guarding a factory. *Madame XX* would have had Donald dealing with a seductive ducktress enemy agent who is after secret plans that have been given to Donald.

How to Be a Commando would have featured Goofy in the style of his "How To" series of cartoons basically demonstrating all the wrong things to do. *A House Divided* would have had the Three Little Pigs as defense plant workers. Only Practical Pig uses his salary to buy defense bonds while the other two pigs are conned by the Big Bad Wolf as a black marketeer into buying useless junk and wasting the money that should have supported the war effort.

Democracy would have followed a man named Jones and his family who escape Germany to come to America and learn about the many freedoms guaranteed by the Constitution and the Bill of Rights. *Square World* was meant to be a satire on Nazi conformity where everything had to be made or pressed into a square shape, including people.

Ajax the Stool Pigeon was about a carrier pigeon who suffers from acrophobia but rises to the occasion to defeat a female avian spy and her minions of Nazi vultures and bats to deliver a vital message.

Training and educational films were also started and abandoned, including *Arsenal of Democracy; Defense of the Hemisphere; The House Fly—Public Enemy #1; Control of the Hookworm; Men, Apes and Moron; Basic English and Its Uses* (designed for an educated foreigner with no knowledge of English and reduced the language to a minimum vocabulary of 800 words); *3043 A.D.;* and *Trees and Tree Products.*

Like other projects such as the stories for feature films about the Little Mermaid and Beauty and the Beast that had been started over the decades and abandoned, *The Gremlins* was filed away in the morgue and occasionally reviewed by future generations to see if there was some way of resolving the challenges or looking at the project from a new perspective.

However, unlike other projects, this one still engenders speculation about what the final film might have been like, whether it would have appealed to a wartime audience and beyond since war-related films like *Casablanca* are still considered cinematic treasures today, and whether it would have become a beloved classic Disney animated feature that introduced delightful new Disney cartoon characters or just another outdated oddity of that era like *Victory Through Air Power*.

There are hundreds and perhaps thousands of unmade animated projects in the Disney vaults, but very few of them ever progressed to the development stage of *The Gremlins*. The ingredients all seemed to be there; they just never seemed to hook together in the right pattern. It was joked that the gremlins had cursed the project to protect their secrets.

Even half a century later, the project still has the mystique of a lost treasure that might have added another classic to the Disney legacy. That's one of the reasons it still intrigues people and will continue to do so with each new generation.

Unfortunately, when it came to this film project, not even the magic of Walt Disney himself was enough to overcome gremlin mischief.

CHAPTER EIGHTEEN

The Warner Bros Gremlins

In 1943, as the term "gremlin" for mischievous mythical creatures and their antics became more and more prominently used in magazine articles and general conversation, Roy O. Disney consulted with the Disney legal staff and came to the realization that the Disney studio no longer had control over what had been considered an exclusive property.

Through his sources, Roy learned that Warner Bros, MGM, Universal, and Columbia were all registering titles for future short cartoons using the word "gremlin." Roy approached the Title Registration Committee to convince them that these new titles violated Disney's claim to the word and previously registered titles, but for what Roy later claimed were "technical reasons" the committee ruled against him.

Since the Disney studio had already invested up to $50,000 in their gremlin feature, Roy leveraged his good will with the other studios to try to prevent them from producing gremlin animated shorts.

Walter Lantz, who was working with Universal, agreed to drop his planned cartoons on the subject and withdraw the titles for those proposed animated shorts. MGM's cartoon producer Fred Quimby agreed to do the same and pledged his full cooperation.

Dave Fleischer, a former fierce competitor of the Disney studio, was working at Columbia after having been ousted from his own animation studio by Paramount about a year earlier, said he would try to cooperate, but emphasized he did not have any authority in the matter.

Roy wrote a memo to Walt dated March 25, 1943, that the other cartoon studios agreed to not produce gremlin cartoons, but gave no reason why it was so easy getting them to do so. Probably Disney's close ties with the U.S. military in producing so many films and its classification as a war plant had as much influence as the personal relationship between Roy and the other studios. Roy told Walt:

> Dave Fleischer stated that he did not have the final say in his plant
> but promised his utmost cooperation not to use the title and not to

make pictures on Gremlins. He discovered two story ideas in the preliminary stages of work.

Behind the scenes, Fleischer apparently continued development of the cartoons, perhaps in retaliation of an old grudge against the Disneys who he felt had driven the Fleischer animation studio out of business by forcing them to compete with feature films that drained their finances.

When Roy found out, he wrote personally to Columbia studio president Harry Cohn on April 16, 1943:

> Excuse me for bothering you with this problem. Walt picked up this idea in connection with some RAF flyers many months before it was commonly tossed around in this country. We made a deal with one of them and a working arrangement with the RAF.
>
> Harry, you know Walt and me well enough to realize we wouldn't give two hoots about competition, short subject to short subject. But I am very worried when we start to make a feature that takes us at least a year to produce and costs us at least $600,000 to $800,000—I'm worried at the thought of having a property of this size undermined and hurt by a lot of single reels that may saturate the public's desire to see a "Gremlin" feature and really do us considerable harm in the marketing of it.
>
> If we were where we could drop it, I would rather do that than proceed under such circumstances. However, we are already in pretty close to $50,000; so that is the reason I'm bothering you with this— to earnestly and seriously request that you persuade your cartoon department to drop the "Gremlin" idea.
>
> Sometime the shoe may be on the other foot; and you know us—we'd be more than happy to return the favor.

B.B. Kahane, who became vice president of Columbia in 1938, replied on behalf of Cohn that Columbia would not develop any cartoons about gremlins, and they never did.

Two animated shorts were already too far into production when Roy requested that Warner Bros producer Leon Schlesinger not produce a gremlin short. However, Schlesinger did change the titles to eliminate the word "gremlin." He apparently never told the animation department of the reason for changing the titles, but they complied because he was the boss.

Falling Hare, released on October 30, 1943, was an eight-minute Technicolor Warner Bros animated short directed by Bob Clampett. Originally the cartoon was entitled *Bugs Bunny and the Gremlin*. The new title was a reference to Bugs falling to earth as a pun on the phrase "falling hair," indicating approaching baldness.

Bob Clampett was a huge Disney fan. He later poked fun at Disney's *Fantasia* (1940) in his Warner Bros cartoon *A Corny Concerto* (1943) and *Snow White and the Seven Dwarfs* in *Coal Black and De Sebben Dwarfs* (1943).

As a teenager, Clampett came up with the rough design sketches of Mickey Mouse after watching Mickey cartoons in a local Glendale movie theater over and over so that his "Aunt" Charlotte Clark could use them to make the first stuffed Mickey Mouse dolls.

He never knew the reason Schlesinger requested the change in the titles to his two gremlin cartoons until 1976 when interviewer Milt Gray told him about Roy Disney's request.

The film's story was unique because Bugs Bunny was the victim rather than the victor and the Oscar-winning rabbit never says "What's up, Doc?" during the entire cartoon. The gremlin wears a blue pilot helmet with short yellow airplane wings extending on either side. He also wears red workman gloves.

During World War II, on an Army airfield, Bugs is relaxing on top of a bomb waiting to be placed into a nearby bomber plane. He is reading a book entitled *Victory Thru Hare Power* (a reference to the 1942 book *Victory Through Airpower* by Major Alexander de Seversky that was the inspiration for a Disney propaganda film). The book claims that gremlins wreck American planes through diabolical sabotage.

Bugs laughingly dismisses such a claim until he sees one of the creatures striking a mallet on the head of a bomb in hopes of detonating it. "These blockbuster bombs don't go off unless you hit them...juuuust right," explains the gremlin to the curious Bugs.

Bugs offers to assist the little creature with his task, using one mighty blow instead of several tiny ones. At almost the last moment, he comes to a shocking realization that the bomb could blow up and stops his swing. The gremlin then hits the rabbit with a monkey wrench. Bugs chases the gremlin onto the bomber and finds himself locked inside as the creature gets the craft airborne.

Throughout the flight, the gremlin physically torments Bugs. At one point, he aims the plane at some skyscrapers and Bugs grabs the controls to roll the plane into a vertical position to fly through them to avoid impact. The plane goes into a tailspin with its wings ripping off and only the fuselage remaining as it plunges toward the ground. However, just before the impact, the plane sputters to a halt just a few feet from the earth.

Both Bugs and the gremlin tell the audience that they ran out of gas because of the "A card," a rationing sticker indicating the lowest priority and limiting the amount of gas purchased to three to four gallons per week. It was a situation familiar to an American wartime audience and resulted in a big laugh of recognition as the final punch line.

The story was credited to Warren Foster, with Rod Scribner as the lead animator.

This particular gremlin makes two reappearances in the *Tiny Toon Adventures* syndicated television series, including the episode "Journey to the Center of Acme Acres" where the gremlin appears (with several look-alikes) as the cause of earthquakes there.

He also appeared in *Night Ghoulery* menancing Plucky Duck in the segment "Gremlin on a Wing," a parody of the iconic *Twilight Zone* television episode "Nightmare at 20,000 Feet" (1963) that featured perhaps the best-known frightening aeronautical gremlin.

In that *Twilight Zone* episode, William Shatner is a nervous passenger on a plane who is the only one who sees a destructive, hairy gremlin (Nick Cravat) tearing at the outside engine and wing. It was later redone as a segment of Warner Bros' *Twilight Zone: The Movie* (1983) with John Lithgow as the passenger who sees a gremlin (Larry Cedar) on the wing.

In a 1975 class, *Twilight Zone* producer Rod Serling stated how he arranged to have a huge blow-up of the gremlin stuck outside writer Richard Matheson's window for a flight they were making together, only to have the prop wash blow it away before he could see it.

Matheson wrote the original short story for his anthology *Alone by Night* (1961), inspired by an actual flight he took, and wrote the screenplay for the television episode. His story and its malevolent gremlin have been referenced in many other television shows, including *The Simpsons, 3rd Rock from the Sun, Saturday Night Live, Robot Chicken*, and *Johnny Bravo*.

The animated gremlin from the Bugs Bunny cartoon also makes a brief cameo, as a passenger, in an *Animaniacs* television episode, "Plane Pals."

Some of the same airplane gags were later recycled in the Bugs Bunny cartoon *Hare Lift* (1952), with Bugs bedeviling Yosemite Sam.

Russian Rhapsody, released on May 20, 1944, was a seven-minute Technicolor Warner Bros animated short directed by Bob Clampett. Originally, the cartoon was entitled *Gremlins from the Kremlin* and the animated short still includes a song by that name sung to the tunes of "*Ochi Chyornye*" ("Dark Eyes") and "*Eh, Uchnem*" ("Song of the Volga Boatmen").

The film's story is a simple framework on which to hang a non-stop series of visual gags. Interestingly, the film makes clear that it is telling a story that is taking place in 1941 rather than in 1944.

During World War II, German bombers are mysteriously disappearing and failing to make it to Moscow to bomb the Soviets into submission. Apparently, colorful Soviet gremlins are sabotaging the planes before their reach their target.

Adolf Hitler is so irate that he decides to fly a bomber "in person" to attack the Russians since he is the best pilot in the world. In flight, the gremlins sneak onto the plane and proceed to dismantle it with hammers, saws, blowtorches, and other tools as they sing that they are "the little men that weren't there." They viciously destroy different parts of the aircraft with unabashed glee.

Hitler discovers the intruders and unsuccesfully tries to stop them as they physically humilate him. Finally, the gremlins cut a hole in the fuselage and drop him out into the sky.

The frightened falling dictator realizes that the plane is now in a power dive aimed right at him. When he reaches the ground he tries to hide, but the plane drives Hitler deep into the ground with the tail section remaining visible and becoming a makeshift tombstone. The gremlins celebrate their victory.

The story is officially credited to Lou Lilly, but it is apparent that others supplied gags. The animation was done by Rod Scribner, Robert McKimson, Manny Gould, and Art Davis.

Many of the gremlins are exaggerated caricatures of the Warner Bros animation department staff, including Chuck Jones (small purple gremlin); Bob Clampett (with pick axe); Friz Freleng (small green gremlin with long pointed nose); Melvin "Tubby" Millar (with the tack on his head); Michael Sasanoff, Michael Maltese, Carl Stalling, and Henry Binder (V-shaped black hair); and John Burton and Ray Katz (being hit by the Schlesinger gremlin).

Even producer Leon Schlesinger appears as a gremlin who is shown tapping the heads off of rivets with a hammer as he's being raised by a rope on a hook through the back of his clothes.

Because of its wartime references, especially its depiction of Hitler, this cartoon was rarely shown on television and now appears only in historical retrospectives.

Director Bob Clampett told me he was always surprised that doing this cartoon did not come back to haunt him and find him in front of the House on UnAmerican Activites Committee or on a blacklist.

At the time Russia was an ally with the United States in the battle against the Nazis and in the cartoon the Russian gremlins from the Kremlin were portrayed as sympathetic heroes. Of course, after the war, any previous support of anything connected with Russia was seen as suspect and possible evidence of Communistic leanings.

It took almost four decades before Warner Bros tackled gremlins again. In 1984, it produced a film directed by Joe Dante entitled simply *Gremlins*.

A young man named Billy receives a gift from his father of a strange creature called a mogwai (the Cantonese word for "monster") as a pet and names it Gizmo. The pet comes with three important rules: never expose it to bright lights or sunlight (which will kill it), do not let it get wet, and never feed it after midnight.

Of course, when a glass of water is spilled on the mild-mannered creature it produces a reptilian, evil gremlin named Stripe who continues to multiply and cause death and destruction in the small town of Kingston Falls. While the evil gremlins are in a theater watching Disney's *Snow White and the Seven Dwarfs*, Billy and his girlfriend blow them up, except for Stripe whom Gizmo later helps defeat.

The film was part of the new trend of horror-comedy like *Ghostbusters* (released the same weekend). Dante admitted to reading the Dahl book before making the movie, but later distanced himself, perhaps for legal reasons, from Dahl's work by claiming that his gremlins had significant differences, including appearance and attitude.

In the film the character of Murray Futterman (played by Dick Miller) says:

> It's the same gremlins that brought down our planes in the Big One.... That's right, World War II.

The script was written by Chris Columbus on "spec," but producer Steven Spielberg felt it was so original that it needed to be made into a film. In the original script Gizmo turned into Stripe when the rules were violated, but Spielberg vetoed that idea.

While the film drew some criticism for its violence, it was a huge financial success. Made on an $11 million budget, it grossed more than $150 million theatrically within the first year and another $80 million when released to video in 1985. A merchandising bonanza was also generated by the film.

Gremlins spawned a series of low-budget imitators like *Critters* and *Ghoulies*. It also spawned a 1990 sequel, *Gremlins 2: The New Batch* (released into theaters the same day as Disney's *Dick Tracy*), again directed by Dante and meant to satrize sequels, but it didn't earn the critical or financial success of the original.

In 1990, Warner Bros announced it was developing a *Gremlins*-based animated television series for its syndicated block of afternoon programming, Kids WB.

The project mysteriously disappeared after a pilot was made, probably due to the lack of success of the theatrical sequel. That same year saw the introduction of the Amblin Entertainment produced series *Tiny Toons Adventures* on the Kids WB from Steven Spielberg.

CHAPTER NINETEEN

Disney's Failed Gremlins Revival

Disney television animation executive Gary Randolph Krisel told *Broadcasting and Cable* magazine in its November 15, 1993 issue:

> Everyone was telling us not to do [a Disney Afternoon cartoon block], that we were crazy if we thought we could reshape the viewing habits of the marketplace. The conventional wisdom during the early 1990s was that it was a boys' action marketplace, with such shows as *G.I. Joe* and *Transformers* dominating the ratings.
>
> Our belief and experience with the Disney library product has been that it holds a timeless and universal appeal with both boys and girls, the latter of which had been almost completely ignored in the late 1970s and early 1980s.
>
> It all pretty much started when I was sitting in [Michael] Eisner's living room with a dish of Gummi Bears sitting on the coffee table. Eisner remarked that his kids couldn't stop eating the candy. We started making up this whole myth and legend about this funny-looking candy. The show that developed scored healthy demographic ratings among boys and girls and went on to a four-year run [1985–1988] before going into syndication.
>
> It gave us the confidence to swing for the fences in the potentially lucrative syndication market with *DuckTales* (1986) with the then-unheard of production cost of $350,000 to $400,000 per episode. The show ranked atop all kids programming, with 7–9 rating averages among key boys and girls demos. By the time we got to our second show with *Chip'n'Dale Rescue Rangers*, there was no doubt we could do it in an hour block with *DuckTales*.

Jeffrey Katzenberg looked through existing Disney properties that could be developed into a series for the Disney Afternoon and came across material on the gremlins.

A memo to Jeff Katzenberg dated March 2, 1990, stated:

Given our rights to Dahl's book as well as the public domain nature of the underlying folklore, we could develop a television show using Dahl's gremlin characters.

The existence of Spielberg's movie, however, presents significant problems in using "The Gremlins" as part or all of the title of such a show.

The Spielberg movie referred to in the memo was the 1984 comedy horror film *Gremlins* directed by Joe Dante. In 1990 Warner Bros had announced it was developing a *Gremlins* animated television series for its Kids WB afternoon animation block of shows and that effectively killed any further discussion of Disney developing a series about gremlins for its competing afternoon block of cartoons.

In 1992, Jerry Rees and Steve Paul Leiva started development on a new feature based on the original Dahl gremlins story to be done in live action with animated gremlins. It was to be done by the Disney television animation division, which wanted to expand its offerings beyond the television series they were producing.

Jerry Rees may be most familiar to people as the director of the animated feature *The Brave Little Toaster* (1987), but he had a varied career on many Disney projects. He was trained at California Institute of the Arts and was mentored by long-time Disney animator Eric Larson.

Rees first worked as an animator on *The Small One* (1978) and then on *The Fox and the Hound* (1981). He later moved on to supervising and creating visual effects for *Tron* (1982). He got frustrated at Disney and left to direct the animated feature *The Brave Little Toaster*.

He returned as a freelance consultant and pitched a gremlins movie, which he saw as a mixture of live action and animation with only the gremlins being animated. In this way, it would make the film more cost effective and emphasize the difference in the gremlins.

Rees' pitch began:

> GREMLINS—The myth of Gremlins that evolved during WWII was actually not a myth—it was Reality. And there are two people alive who know about it....

It would have been a "retro" film taking place during the 1940s with a handsome young pilot and his attractive girlfriend as the main characters.

Steve Moore and Frans Vischer did some design work that was completely different from the original vintage Bill Justice designs and different from the reptilian Warner Bros creations.

The final design was what Moore called "ameboid" figures that were "somewhere between spirits and real creatures." They had bulbous bald heads, except for three multi-colored strands on the top, and protruding sharp, pointy lips.

They were unclothed and a single bright blue color, although other pitch artwork showed a variety of other bright colors and that they could morph into different shapes like a drop of mercury. They could open portals in their bodies to make musical sounds. The pitch board described it as:

> A celebration begins. A Gremlin band performs exhilarating "wind music." Sort of an aboriginal pan pipe/jug band/calliope sound!

The intent was that they lived in the upper atmosphere clouds and were slender, elegant blue figures made of moisture, but as they got closer to earth, air pressure and gravity transformed them into squat blobs. When they hit the windows of planes they looked like big raindrops splattering against the glass.

Rees pitched the idea to Katzenberg who liked it but felt it might be too complicated and expensive.

When this proposal was dismissed, Rees and Leiva went on to work on a Betty Boop animated feature film at MGM that got cancelled at the last minute.

The Disney gremlins were given a new life in the world of video games.

When Warren Spector was given access to the Disney archives as he was developing the platform video game *Epic Mickey* released in November 2010, he found the characters of Gremlin Gus and the other gremlins there, and decided to make Gremlin Gus a main focal point of the game as Mickey's "spirit guide." Spector stated:

> If you need a guide through the wilds of Wasteland, you couldn't do better than Gus the Gremlin. The Gremlins have been kept tightly under wraps thanks to the machinations of the Mad Doctor, but Gus manages to escape the Doc's clutches just in time to aid Mickey on his quest to save Wasteland.

> Possessed of magical powers, copious knowledge of every aspect of Wasteland, and a crisp British accent, Gus the Gremlin is a totally dedicated and unswervingly loyal companion who can help steer any quest to a successful conclusion...especially when the future of an entire world hinges upon it!

In the *Epic Mickey* video game, Gremlin Gus serves as a constant guide to Mickey Mouse through the Cartoon Wasteland. Of course, he is still the leader of the gremlins and there is a Gremlin Village that includes discarded parts from the "it's a small world" Disney theme park attraction. He never formally introduces himself to Mickey, except in the online game, *Epic Mickey: Path Painter.*

Gus is used to explain to Mickey what is going on, where he is, and to give advice. He shows Mickey how to travel between different sections and tells him the story of Oswald the Rabbit. Gus and Mickey develop a friendship.

The gremlins of the Wasteland are similar to their original source material—scrappy, resourceful, and mechanically savvy. They use these skills to keep the rides and buildings of Wasteland in good repair, although it is a constant struggle.

Lead artist and animator Jorma Auburn stated:

> We tried various personalities for the Gremlins as there was a lot of wiggle room for them. We went from uber cute to totally zany and found a happy, charming middle of the road for them.

Gus returns to help Mickey in *Epic Mickey 2: The Power of Two*, released in November 2012. Once again, Gus teaches Mickey the ways and history of the Cartoon Wasteland. The poor reception to the sequel resulted in the franchise being put on indefinite hiatus, even though there had been some development on a third installment.

For those gamers unfamiliar with the original source material, the developers compared Gremlin Gus with Papa Smurf not only because of a physical resemblance but also some similarities between the world of the Smurfs and the world of the gremlins.

The Dark Horse Gremlins Revival

Dark Horse Comics was founded in 1986 by publisher Mike Richardson. While the company has many popular original titles, it also found great success in producing comics with licensed properties including *Star Wars*, *Buffy the Vampire Slayer*, *Alien*, and *Predator*.

The company expanded in 1992 to include the production of television shows and films like *The Mask* (1994), *Hellboy* (2004), and *Sin City* (2005). In 1998, Dark Horse launched a branch of the company to create toys, apparel, model kits, and other merchandise.

In 2006, Dark Horse saw the opportunity to revive Disney's long-dormant gremlins. The game plan was to produce new comic books and merchandise and hopefully jump-start a new franchise.

Mike Richardson first heard about the gremlins from film historian Leonard Maltin's commentary on the DVD Walt Disney Treasures set *On the Front Lines*, dealing with the Disney studio animation work during World War II.

He was intrigued by the concept of Dahl and Disney working together, that Dahl's first book had never been reprinted, and by the appealing designs of the characters.

After purchasing a copy of the original 1943 storybook, he had Anita Nelson, Dark Horse's vice president of licensing, contact the Disney company about licensing the characters. The people they contacted at Disney had no idea they owned the characters or the rights to the original Dahl book.

Dark Horse had to convince Disney to re-check their files again more thoroughly. Everyone finally agreed that Disney did indeed own the property and could license it to Dark Horse. The next hurdle came down to figuring out how the project should be approached.

Richardson said:

> We have a great relationship with Disney. Generally, this particular project was similar to others in that Disney took great care in the

approval process to make sure that the characters and plot were consistent with company guidelines.

Specifically, however, they wanted the property moved away from the military element present in Dahl's original book. The trick was to try to keep the basic story and character continuity alive and at the same time invent a new environment and purpose for the Gremlins.

David Scroggy, who was the vice president of product development for Dark Horse at the time, stated:

> The Disney Gremlins have a timeless quality, and getting a chance to recreate their world is an honor. They have a heritage and a history that you don't find very often. The modern interpretation of gremlins is quite a bit different from the illustrations by Disney animation artist Bill Justice, but the concept of them has been with our culture for over half a century.
>
> Dark Horse is great at seeing opportunities in properties, new and old, that have been overlooked. We knew this was another one of those situations. *The Gremlins* is a great story with a lot of potential. Disney's George McClements was our primary contact for approval on the Gremlins merchandise project, and Tonya Agurto steered the publishing deal.

On September 26, 2006, Dark Horse released a reprint of the original 1943 book at the affordable price of $12.95 that is still in print and available for purchase. Even battered copies of the rare first edition were selling at the time for hundreds of dollars, and sometimes over $1,000, so this reprint was a much-welcomed edition for Disney fans.

Unfortunately, like many reprints of classic books, like the Frank Thomas and Ollie Johnston's *Disney Animation: The Illusion of Life* (1984), the original layout material no longer existed, so a copy of the actual book had to be photographed in order to be duplicated and then digitally restored for the reprint edition.

In the case of *The Gremlins*, this resulted in the bright colors of the original color illustrations being somewhat muted in the reprint. The image of Gremlin Gus on the joystick in the original shows the instrument dials as clearly legible, which is not the case in the Dark Horse edition.

Dark Horse Deluxe also created a line of toys to tie in with the book, the first time Disney gremlins toys had been made available in decades.

Scroggy said:

> The Dark Horse PVC sets, large vinyl figures and limited-edition figurines are intended to represent the Gremlins doing what they do best: causing havoc.

Although they destroyed planes in the book, we made a point of picking poses that would make as much sense sitting on your desk as they would on the wing of a plane. Many of the poses were directly from the original Bill Justice book illustrations.

Working side by side with Disney Consumer Products and Gentle Giant Studios, Dark Horse Deluxe released a two-pack of vinyl figures. Standing seven inches tall, Gremlin Gus and Fifinella, the main male and female characters from the book, were packaged in one set released January 24, 2007, with a retail price of $34.99.

Scroggy continued:

Gremlins don't have a specific skin tone; they come in every color of the rainbow. Fifinellas are always the same—color them beautiful! You can pick any color you want and claim that it is correct, but we wanted to find colors that worked well with each other and gave them an animated feel.

With the figures, we wanted to create as much subtlety in the paint as we could. The colors are simple, so we chose to mix matte and gloss paint. Most would overlook details like that, but those are the types of details that we take pride in.

In addition, Dark Horse Deluxe released nine gremlins PVC figures in three sets on November 29, 2006, for $14.99 apiece. Each character was approximately three inches tall and was gleefully using various implements of destruction to saw, carve, hammer, and perform other acts of mischief.

- The Jamface Set had one gremlin in a green helmet with a pick axe raised above his head, one in a red helmet with a huge nail that he is using to scratch an imprint, and one in an orange helmet using a hand drill.

- The Rufus Set had two gremlins with purple and green helmets using a cross-cut saw. Another gremlin in an orange helmet was jauntily carrying two over-filled buckets of water that was sloshing over the top.

- The Gremlin Gus Set had a yellow-helmeted gremlin riding on a jackhammer, a red-helmeted Gremlin Gus covering both his ears with his hands and an expression of annoyance, and a blue helmeted gremlin with a hammer.

In addition, three special limited-edition polyresin statuettes were produced retailing at $44.95 each: Gremlin with Pipe (featuring a 3½-inch tall gremlin looking curiously into the bowl of a human's unlit smoking pipe), Fifinella and Widgits (featuring Fifinella taking care of three Widgits, one of whom has started to float off the ground), and Gremlin with Postage Stamp (featuring a smiling gremlin taking a bite out of a replica of a 1939

Eiffel Tower postage stamp because, according to Dahl, gremlins liked to eat the glue on the back of stamps). Two 11- to 12-inch-tall plush dolls of Gremlin Gus and Fifinella were also produced.

A three-issue comic book series was released in 2007 written by Mike Richardson and set in the modern world rather than during World War II. Richardson said:

> Once we learned that Disney wanted Gremlins updated, I pulled rank and decided to write the series myself. I tried to make the project feel like a classic Disney story, complete with love interest and a well defined, if two-dimensional, villain. The story itself fell into place pretty easily. I looked at the promise Gus made in the original book (for the gremlins to stay in his house near a forest) and went from there.

> I'm a long-time fan of all things Walt Disney and at the same time well aware of Roald Dahl's children's books. The idea that the two men had actually hung out and even collaborated on this project intrigued me more than I can say. The bottom line is that once the opportunity presented itself, it was mine.

Dark Horse released a plot summary when the first issue was published:

> Our story opens on Gus, a man visiting England from the States. His grandfather's house is part of his inheritance, and he plans to sell it as soon as he can.

> Even though the locals think the house is haunted—something Gus immediately dismisses—a slick man named Mr. Snide promptly appears with his "associates" and makes an offer.

> But when Gus declines to sign over the house right then and there, Snide reveals that his arrangement with the mayor will seal the deal soon enough!

> Left to explore the place, Gus experiences a series of very odd events. How did his folded clothes end up in knots? Who on earth would drill a hole in a coffee cup? Certainly not ghosts, but for a former fighter pilot's abandoned old home, it sure is clean....

> When the house's tiny residents decide to take extreme measures, Gus will meet the gremlins up close and personal-just like his grandfather, who first discovered them 60 years ago!

The artist for the series was cartoonist and animator Dean Yeagle, perhaps best known for his playful young woman character Mandy, who appeared in the pages of *Playboy* magazine.

However, once again the curse struck and Yeagle was unable to finish the series and so Fabio Laguna, an artist for Dreamworks Consumer Products, was brought in to finish the final issue.

Yeagle stated that it was originally Richardson's idea to revive the Disney gremlins. To tempt Yeagle, they sent him the storyboards that were prepared by Disney for the original never-made film.

Yeagle told interviewer Jake Friedman:

> They're great little designs and very pleasant to draw. The comic book that I'm working on is a sequel to the original. When Dark Horse wanted to put out a new printing of the old book Disney said, "OK, but we want to also put out a three-issue comic book showing what happened to them afterward, in today's age."

> It was written by Mike Richardson and I'm doing the first two issues out of the three. I was going to do the whole thing, but time and moving and other work got in the way, and I've only been able to do the first two, although I did all the covers. There are new human characters, which are all my designs, but the gremlins are all the same ones from the book. They live a long time.

> Well, they're not working on planes anymore. In the original story the air force came in and built aircraft factories in their woods. So they were so angry they started wrecking the airplanes. And the lead flyer came to an agreement with them to stop wrecking the airplanes, and let them live in the big house that he had, which is where they're living now.

> In our story, they find out that their house might be sold, and they begin to wreak havoc again, on the more villainous characters. So they're still up to their old tricks, but they don't do them to planes; they do them to houses, cars and things.

> Disney was pretty hands-off, except I was approved by Disney to do this. I am in their database as an approved Disney artist, which was actually news to me, but Dark Horse found that out. And I have a reasonably free hand with what I can do.

Return of the Gremlins #1 (March 2008)

A 20-page story written by Mike Richardson and drawn by Dean Yeagle. Young Gus, an American tire salesman, shows up to sell his late grandfather's house that is supposedly haunted. Mr. Snide seems overly eager to purchase the property that also includes forest acreage. Gus discovers that the strange noises and odd activities in the house are the result of gremlins. Also included is a reprint of a six-page comic book retelling of Dahl's original story from the Dell comic book *War Heroes* (April–June 1943).

Return of the Gremlins #2 (April 2008)

In another 20-page story written by Richardson and drawn by Yeagle, the gremlins mistakenly think that Young Gus has come to save the house and the forest land that was promised to them by his grandfather. Young Gus meets Mister Bolton, a friend of his grandfather, who knows about the gremlins.

Bolton has an attractive redheaded daughter named Molly, a local librarian around the same age as Young Gus who has also helped take care of the gremlins for years along with her father.

The local mayor shows up claiming that the property has unpaid back taxes and fees and that the city has exercised its right of eminent domain to seize the property. Mr. Snide eagerly mounts a bulldozer to level the property to the ground.

In addition, there are three two-page wordless gremlin stories written and drawn by cartoonist Walt Kelly, reprinted from three different 1944 issues of the Dell comic book *Walt Disney's Comics and Stories* (Nos. 38, 40, and 41).

Return of the Gremlins #3 (May 2008)

In this 20-page story written by Richardson and drawn by new artist Fabio Laguna, Young Gus is arrested and taken to jail as he attempts to stop his grandfather's house from being bulldozed to the ground. The gremlins follow him and break him out of jail.

Back at the property, the gremlins steal the bulldozer and, pretending to be ghosts, scatter people away.

Young Gus returns to City Hall begging to be locked up to save him from the ghosts that Mr. Snide has stirred up with his bulldozers. The rest of the citizenry, after seeing odd things in town, quickly agree that the property should be left alone.

Mr. Snide, who has claimed all along not to believe in ghosts but desperately wants the property for a development deal, returns to the house where he is confronted by the gremlins in person and is scared away. Young Gus decides to stay and get better acquainted with the gremlins, and with Molly.

Additional material included a two-page comic book tale of the gremlins drawn by Vive Rito and reprinted from *Walt Disney Comics and Stories* No. 34 (1943) and two more two-page Walt Kelly wordless gremlin stories from WDCS Nos. 37 and 39. There is also a reprint of the cover of *WDCS* Vol. 3, No. 10 (July 1943) of Walt Kelly's illustration of Donald Duck in a red airplane and wielding a fly swatter to battle the mischief of six gremlins.

A book signing of the comics was held at the Disney Soda Fountain on Hollywood Boulevard in Los Angeles, California, on March 19, 2008. Yeagle and Richardson were in attendance along with Leonard Maltin, who wrote the introduction for the reprint hardcover and had just released a new book, *Leonard Maltin's Movie Crazy*.

A hardcover collection of the three comic books and supplemental material was published June 2015.

Richardson said:

> I love all of the items we've created including both the books and toys. It's really been a fun project to bring these characters back. My office at home has Gremlins running around all over the furniture.
>
> It's really been interesting to find out how many people didn't realize where the gremlins came from and the connection between Disney and Dahl. When people see and ask about them, I love telling the whole story.

Lack of a movie or television tie-in as well as general awareness of the characters once again sealed the fate of the tiny creatures.

The Disney Studio's War Cartoons: 1942–1943

In addition to dozens of training and technical films, these were the cartoons that the Disney studio produced when the Gremlins project was being developed.

Notably, the Disney films of these years did not feature racist caricatures of the Japanese as was common from other animation studios hoping to stir feelings in audiences about the sneak attack on Pearl Harbor, like the 1942 cartoons featuring Popeye in *You're a Sap, Mr. Jap* and Daffy Duck in *The Ducktators*.

The Disney cartoons exuded American self-confidence, a sense of hope, and even some appropriate humor. They are listed here alphabetically by year.

1942

The Army Mascot (5/22/42). Pluto finds himself in Camp Drafty where he sees the army mascots receiving healthy portions of delicious rations. He inadvertently eats a goat's plug of tobacco and when the goat tries to ram the poor pup, he finds himself embedded in a passing Yankee Clipper. The next day, Pluto is the new mascot of the "Yoo Hoo" Division eagerly awaiting his delivery from a meat truck as he salutes with his ear.

Donald Gets Drafted (5/1/42). Donald "Fauntleroy" Duck (the first and only time Donald's middle name is revealed) proceeds to Draft Board No. 13 located on the corner of Soldiers Walk and Generals Drive. He goes through an extensive and humiliating series of physical examinations and then finds himself under the supervision of Sergeant Pete who is irritated by Donald's lack of discipline. Some agonizing ants trigger Donald's temper while he is standing at attention and results in his firing his rifle at Pete. Donald ends up behind bars surrounded by a huge stack of potatoes to peel.

Food Will Win the War (7/2/42) Done for the Department of Agriculture about the importance of farmers to the war effort and to give encouragement to our hard-fighting but underfed allies that food would soon be coming, the short showed the sacrifices being made by American farmers and the dangers in delivering the food to our allies.

The New Spirit (1/23/42). Listening intently to the radio for the latest war news, Donald Duck finds himself inspired by a plea to pay his taxes to beat the Axis. Donald quickly fills out his tax form and rushes across country to personally deliver his thirteen-dollar check. This is followed by animation showing how coins can mount up quickly resulting in the sinking of an enemy warship. Other similar images follow in a montage reinforcing the importance of tax money to defeat the enemy. Produced for the U.S. Treasury, this short had 11,700 bookings in the six weeks prior to tax day (which at that time was March 15) with many theaters booking it for free rather than paying for a regular Disney commercial short.

Out of the Frying Pan Into the Fire (7/24/42). A three-minute animated cartoon made for the War Production Board. It features Minnie Mouse and Pluto and explains why it is necessary to save fats like bacon grease to make glycerin for explosives. Initially, Pluto is upset he won't get a tasty treat, but when a montage shows how the waste fat will give "a boy at the front an extra clip of cartridges" and a quick shot of a framed photo of Mickey Mouse in uniform, Pluto is inspired to sacrifice. "One pound of grease can make five [cannon] shells." Pluto gets rewarded—with a string of wienies—for taking a can of grease to the local butcher shop.

Sky Trooper (11/6/42). Private Donald Duck is peeling potatoes at the Mallard Field Air Training Base, but longs to take to the skies. Sergeant Pete gives him a parachute and tells him to board a nearby plane. Once in the air, Donald chickens out from bailing like the rest of the soldiers. He scrambles with Pete in the plane and they both find themselves falling out of the plane holding onto a bomb. They try to get away from it, but it makes a direct hit on the general's headquarters. Both in extensive bandages from their injuries, Donald and Pete peel stacks of potatoes as punishment.

The Vanishing Private (9/25/42). Sergeant Pete is unhappy with Private Duck using polka-dot paint to camouflage a large cannon. Donald finds some experimental "invisible paint" and uses it instead. Pete returns and believes the gun to have been stolen since he can't see it. Donald pokes his head out of the invisible barrel and in the ensuing melee is covered with the paint. Pete chases after the invisible duck with grenades. They run into a general and the invisible duck has some fun. The final shot is a visible Donald marching past a padded cell where Pete is being held for acting crazy.

1943

Chicken Little (12/17/43). Foxy Loxy can't get into the farmyard because of its defenses so he reads a book (originally intended to be Adolf Hitler's *Mein Kampf* but changed to a generic book entitled *Psychology*). The clever fox uses the book's advice to undermine the farm animals' faith in their leader, Cocky-Locky. He then tricks the yo-yo playing simpleton Chicken Little into thinking the sky is falling and leading the flock into the fox's cave for safety. The last scene is the fox picking his teeth and surrounded by a graveyard full of chicken wish bones. The cartoon with this shocking ending was meant to warn against rumors and enemy propaganda and was made under contract with the Coordinator of Inter-American Affairs (CIAA).

Defense Against Invasion (8/5/43). Four young boys in a doctor's office are worried about being vaccinated. The doctor calms their fears by showing them that their bodies are like a city that could be overrun by invading germs, but that vaccinations are the ammunition needed to repel the invaders. "V for Vaccination and Victory. Victory over Invasion." The short was a mix of animation and live action.

Der Fuehrer's Face (1/1/43). This cartoon won an Academy Award for Best Cartoon of 1942, even though it was officially released in 1943. Donald Duck dreams he lives in a surrealistic Nazi Germany. The original title for the film was *Donald Duck in Axis Land* and later *Donald Duck in Nutziland*. Donald works in a munitions factory where he tightens the fuse caps on shells while constantly being forced to heil [salute]. The strain of it all drives him berserk, but he awakes in his bed to find it was all just a nightmare and is comforted by his nearby model of the Statue of Liberty.

Education for Death (1/15/43). Based on the Gregor Ziemer book *Education for Death: The Making of a Nazi,* the film shows how the youth of Germany is indoctrinated into becoming good Nazis who burn books, sack churches, and despise culture through a representative young boy named Hans. He does not belong to his parents, but to the state. He finally marches along with other young soldiers as they dissolve into markers in a cemetery.

Fall Out, Fall In (4/23/43). G.I. Donald Duck is marching with his platoon through threatening weather, from snow and ice to desert heat. It takes him almost all night to set up his uncooperative pup tent and when he finally falls asleep, the dawn has come again and he must march some more.

The Grain That Built a Hemisphere (1/4/43). This short tells the story of corn and how it has spread and influenced the culture and economic structure of the world. The film helps explains the importance of corn for feeding livestock and for providing starches, alcohol, plastics, and explosives.

Home Defense (11/26/43). "Front Admiral" Donald Duck and his nephews attired in outrageous military uniforms man their homemade coastal listening post to spot enemy planes. After Donald falls asleep, the nephews trick him into believing there is an enemy attack with paratroops. When Donald realizes he has been fooled, he drums his nephews out of the service but quickly calls them back when he thinks he hears a real invasion which turns out to be a buzzing bee caught in his listening device. Thinking he is hearing a plane, Donald orders the nephews to fire the cannon to the coordinates, blowing up the amplifier and Donald himself.

The Old Army Game (11/5/43). Sergeant Pete discovers his soldiers have snuck out of camp. He catches Donald Duck trying to sneak back into the barracks and the usual hijinks ensue, including a macabre gag where Donald believes he has been cut in half. (He hasn't.)

Private Pluto (4/2/43). Pluto is warned to beware of saboteurs when he is on guard duty of a turreted coastal gun emplacement. He runs into two chipmunks who are using the cannon barrel to store and crack nuts. Pluto tries to evict them, but they continue to outsmart him throughout the cartoon. Although they are drawn fairly generically, the chipmunks are obviously prototypes for the later Chip'n'Dale.

Reason and Emotion (8/27/43). The short demonstrates the struggle in the human brain between uncontrolled and irrational primitive emotion and the more intelligent and sophisticated reason. These aspects are personified as a caveman and a bespectacled, proper gentleman in a suit. The end of the film shows that both need to work together to win the war.

The Spirit of '43 (1/7/43). Donald Duck is a factory worker who, on payday, is torn between two desires for the money he has earned, as personified by a thrifty Scottish duck and a zoot-suited spendthrift duck who urges Donald to spend it on drinks and a couple of dates at the sleazy Idle Hours Club. Donald realizes that what he needs to do is rush to the IRS to make an advance payment on his taxes. The rest of the film repeats footage from the previous year's *The New Spirit*. The film was distributed theatrically by the Treasury Department.

Victory Through Air Power (8/13/43). The history of aviation is briefly shown in a humorous animated segment and then the career of Major Alexander de Seversky is summarized. DeSeversky appears in live action explaining the importance of using aircraft for victory, especially strategic long-range bombing.

It is a fairly straight feature-length documentary-type film based on DeSeversky's book of the same name and produced completely by the Disney studio with no support from the military.

In fact, Walt was risking future government contracts as some branches of the armed forces, including the Navy, Disney's biggest military client, tried to talk Walt out of making the film because they disagreed with the premise. The Navy felt that battleships would win the war.

Besides the opening history of aviation, there is also striking use of animation in the live-action section that includes the memorable image of a Japanese octopus expanding its influence and being attacked by an American eagle to relinquish territory from its tentacled grip. There had been some initial discussion in the planning stages to use Mickey Mouse and Donald Duck, but they did appear in advertising and promotional material for the film, though not in the film itself.

Victory Through Air Power lost $436,000, but Walt was convinced it was a film that needed to be made. Roy Disney said, "We did it as a patriotic gesture."

Prime Minister Winston Churchill was so impressed with the film that he had a copy brought by fighter jet to the Quebec Conference in August 1943 to show President Franklin D. Roosevelt. After seeing it, Roosevelt ordered the film to be shown to the Joint Chiefs of Staff and it undoubtedly helped influence American air strategy for the rest of the war.

Victory Vehicles (7/30/43). Using Goofy, the cartoon illustrates some wildly imaginative alternative methods of transportation, since cars, gas, and tires were in short supply because of war-time needs.

Water, Friend or Enemy (5/1/43). A narrator explains how to prevent the pollution of drinking water and its contamination by diseases such as cholera, typhoid, and dysentery. Clever use of animation effects were employed, including sliding cels, dissolves, and wash-offs.

The Winged Scourge (1/15/43). The famous Seven Dwarfs from *Snow White* demonstrate the precautions needed to safeguard homes from mosquitoes and how to prevent the spread of malaria.

Disney Military Training Films 1942-1943

The running times refer to the Disney-produced footage and are sometimes *not* the total running time of the finished film itself, which may have just included a segment made by Disney.

For instance, Disney produced eight minutes of animation for a U.S. Army project entitled *Battle of Britain*, but the actual film runs fifty-three minutes with the additional live action. For *The Nazi Strike (Campaign in Poland)*, Disney produced thirteen minutes of animation, but the actual production runs forty-one minutes.

Production numbers refer to the numbers that the Disney studio used and may not align with the production numbers that the military assigned to the film.

The Disney studio was not allowed to keep any material used in the making of the film (like layouts or finished cels) or the film itself because it was considered classified material. Even story meeting notes were incinerated.

These are the known and confirmed productions. They are listed here alphabetically by year. Other films were discussed, started, and abandoned, and some even produced with no reliable reference existing for confirmation.

1942

- Aircraft Carrier Landing Signals (U.S. Navy) 15 min. (Prod. 2616)
- Aircraft Carrier Mat Approaches and Landings (U.S. Navy) 14 min. (Prod. 2617)
- Aircraft Riveting (U.S. Navy) 23 min. (Prod. 2629)
- Approaches and Landings (U.S. Navy) 17 min. (Prod. 2624)

- Battle of Britain (U.S. Army) 8 min. (Prod. 2640)
- Bending and Curving (U.S. Navy) 37 min. (Prod. 2631)
- Blanking and Punching (U.S. Navy) 24 min. (Prod. 2633)
- Forming Methods (U.S. Navy) 40 min. (Prod. 2627)
- Icing Conditions (U.S. Navy) 40 min. (Prod. 2623)
- Know Your Enemy—Germany (U.S. Army) 2 min. (Prod. 2647, 4029)
- The Nazis Strike (Campaign in Poland) (U.S. Army) 13 min. (Prod. 4003)
- Prelude to War (U.S. Army) 16 min. (Prod. 4024)
- Protection Against Chemical Warfare (U.S. Navy) 9 min. (Prod. 2625)
- U.S. Army Identification Series—WEFT (U.S. Army) 11 different parts made for a total of 101 min. (Prod. 2615)
- U.S. Navy Identification Series—WEFT (U.S. Navy) 13 different parts made for a total of 73 min. (Prod. 2609)
- U.S. Navy Identification—3 Point System, Warships (U.S. Navy) 38 different parts made for a total of 135 min. (Prod. 2609)

1943

- Aeronca Project (Basic Maintenance of Primary Training Airplanes) (U.S. Army and Aeronca Aircraft Corporation) 112 min. (Prod. 2660)
- Air Masses and Fronts (U.S. Navy) 25 min. (Prod. 2650)
- Air Transport Command (U.S. Army) 10 min. (Prod. 2678, 2680)
- Aircraft Carrier Landing Qualifications (U.S. Navy) 26 min. (Prod. 2618)
- Aircraft Welding (U.S. Navy) unknown min. (Prod. 2635)
- The Aleutian Islands (Alaska Defense Command Project) (U.S. Army) 20 min. (Prod. 2646)
- Battle of China (U.S. Army) unknown min. actual film runs 67 min. (Prod. 2641, 2684, 4002)
- Battle of Russia (War in the East) (U.S. Army) 20 min. of animation but actual film runs 80 min. (Prod. 2671)
- Beechcraft Maintenance and Repair (for Beech Aircraft Corporation and U.S. Army) 13 different parts made for a total of 359 min. (Prod. 2644)
- British Torpedo Plane Tactics (U.S. Navy) 11 min. (Prod. 2626)

- Carrier Rendezvous and Breakup (Aircraft Rendezvous—Aircraft Formation Breakup) (U.S. Navy) 19 min. (Prod. 2662)
- The Cold Front (U.S. Navy) 19 min. (Prod. 2651)
- Divide and Conquer (U.S. Navy) unknown min., actual film runs 60 min. (Prod. 2639)
- Fast Company (U.S. Army) 1 min. (Prod. 2669)
- Fixed Gunnery and Fighter Tactics (Jacksonville Project) (U.S. Navy) 78 min. (Prod. 2648)
- Fog (U.S. Navy) 24 min. (Prod. 2622)
- Glider Training (Research Council Project #343) (U.S. Army) 3 different parts for a total of 17 min. (Prod. 2663)
- Heat Treating (U.S. Navy) 12 min. (Prod. 2630)
- High Level Precision Bombing (Colonel Garland Project) 2 different parts for a total of 61 min. (Prod. 2681)
- Know Your Enemy—Japan (U.S. Army) 18 min. (Prod. 2667, 2676, 4022)
- Lofting and Layouts (U.S. Navy) 30 min. (Prod. 2634)
- The Mark 13—Modification 1 Aerial Torpedo (San Diego Project) (U.S. Navy) 5 different parts for a total of 121 min. (Prod. 2652)
- Minneapolis Honeywell Project (C-1 Auto Pilot) (U.S. Army) 12 different parts for a total of 243 minutes (Prod. 2659)
- Mock-up and Tooling (Aircraft Tooling) (U.S. Navy) 19 min. (Prod. 2628)
- The Occluded Front (U.S. Navy) 30 min. (Prod. 2655)
- Rules of the Nautical Road (U.S. Navy) 26 different parts for a total of 207 min. (Prod. 2620)
- Substitution and Conversion (U.S. Army) 20 min. (Prod. 2668)
- Template Reproduction (U.S. Navy) 18 min. (Prod. 2636)
- Thunderstorms (U.S. Navy) 39 min. (Prod.2621)
- V.T.B. Pilot Training (U.S. Navy) 20 min. (Prod. 2666)
- The Warm Front (U.S. Navy) 20 min. (Prod. 2653)

Selected Bibliography

This book has benefited greatly from the early research of John Cawley, Paul Anderson, Richard Shale, and David Lesjak.

Baxter, John. *Disney During World War II* (Disney Editions 2014).

Cawley, John. "Walt Disney and The Gremlins: An Unfinished Story." *American Classic Screen* (Spring 1980).

Dahl, Roald. *The Gremlins* (Random House 1943, reprint Dark Horse Books 2006).

Dahl, Roald. "Lucky Break." *The Wonderful World of Henry Sugar* (1977).

Justice, Bill. *Justice for Disney* (Tomart 1992).

Justice, Bill. Interview with Jim Korkis (1997).

Korkis, Jim. "The Trouble with Gremlins: The True Story of a Never-Made Disney Animated Classic." *Hogan's Alley* #15 (2007).

Lesjak, David. *Toons at War* (self-published limited edition 2000).

Lesjak, David. *Service with Character* (Theme Park Press 2014).

Maltin, Leonard. "The Gremlins Got 'Em: How Walt Disney and Roald Dahl Didn't Get to Make a Movie Together," in *The Gremlins* (Dark Horse Books 2006).

Rawls, Walton. *Disney Dons Dogtags* (Abbeville Press 1992).

Richardson, Mike. *Walt Disney: Return of the Gremlins* (Dark Horse Books 2015).

Shale, Richard. *Donald Duck Joins Up* (UMI Research Press 1976, 1982).

Solomon, Charles. *The Disney That Never Was* (Hyperion 1995).

Sturrock, Donald. *Storyteller: The Authorized Biography of Roald Dahl* (Simon & Schuster 2010).

Treglown, Jeremy. *Roald Dahl: A Biography* (Farrar, Strauss, Grioux 1994).

Acknowledgments

I thank all of those people who have purchased previous books about Disney history that I have written because it allowed this book to be published as well.

This book would not have been possible without the encouragement of Bob McLain and his Theme Park Press. Bob works a lot harder than anyone suspects producing these obscure Disney history titles that may only sell a handful of copies. His efforts have enriched the world of Disney for us all.

As always, thanks to my two brothers and their families. They are all completely uninterested in the books I write, but as I grow older, I realize more and more the importance of family.

Both my mom and dad served in the military during World War II and it is where they met and then later married after the war was over. I grew up hearing many stories about that time period and military bureaucracy. I still carry with me today the small Bible that my uncle carried with him throughout his service during World War II. I also inherited his Mickey Mouse watch that I still wear today as well.

Special appreciation goes to David Lesjak, an acknowledged expert on Disney during World War II. He has been extremely supportive of my writing this book to the point of loaning me some treasures from his own extensive collection.

I thank all those who have researched and written about Disney history and in doing so have inspired me, with special recognition for this book to John Cawley, Paul Anderson, Richard Shale (whose *Donald Duck Joins Up* still remains invaluable today as a source of accurate information about Disney in World War II), Didier Ghez, Leonard Maltin, Bill Justice, Jerry Beck, and so many others.

Special acknowledgement to the gremlins, whose worst mischief comes when they are not recognized and who continue to inspire a sense of wonder and new tales of mystery.

About the Author

Jim Korkis is an internationally respected Disney historian who has written hundreds of articles and a dozen books about all things Disney over the last thirty-five years.

Jim grew up in Glendale, California, where he was able to meet and interview Walt's original team of animators and Imagineers. In 1995, he relocated to Orlando, Florida, where he worked for Walt Disney World in a variety of capacities, including Entertainment, Animation, Disney Institute, Disney University, College and International Programs, Disney Cruise Line, Disney Design Group, and Marketing.

His original research on Disney history has been used often by the Disney company as well as other organizations such as the Walt Disney Family Museum.

Several websites feature Jim's articles about Disney history:

- MousePlanet.com
- AllEars.net
- Yesterland.com
- CartoonResearch.com
- YourFirstVisit.net

In addition, Jim is a frequent guest on multiple podcasts as well as a consultant and keynote speaker to various businesses and groups.

When Jim worked at Walt Disney World, he was considered a leading expert in WDW history and prepared the questions for the various rounds of the annual cast member WDW trivia competition as well as being the host for the final round.

He also wrote quarterly Disney history columns for the *Disney Vacation Club* magazine, the text for the WDW trading cards, and gave frequent presentations and tours to cast members and WDW corporate partners.

Jim is not currently an employee of the Disney ccompany.

To read more stories by Jim Korkis about Disney history, please check out his other books, all available from Theme Park Press.

More Books from Theme Park Press

Theme Park Press is the largest independent publisher of Disney, Disney-related, and general interest theme park books in the world, with over 100 new releases each year.

We're always looking for new talent.

For a complete catalog, including book descriptions and excerpts, please visit:

ThemeParkPress.com

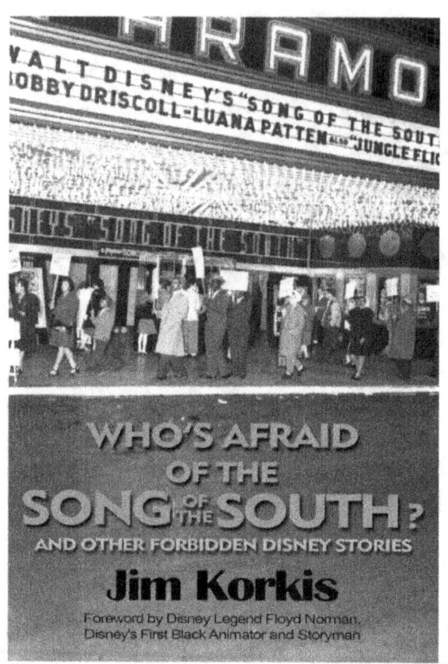

The Dark Side of Disney

You won't find it on cable. You won't find it on NetFlix. Ever. Disney thinks that you can't handle *Song of the South*, a film that Walt Disney himself championed from contentious start to controversial finish. Jim Korkis chronicles the sad ballad of this forbidden film, lynched by the politically correct and banished to the deepest, darkest depths of the Disney vault for its "racist" storyline.

themeparkpress.com/books/song-south.htm

Donald Duck's Other Daddy

Disney animator, storyman, and director Jack Hannah's career with Walt (both Disney and Lantz) spanned decades, beginning with his first job at the Disney studio in 1933, as a clean-up artist. His stories are as memorable as the character he helped define, Donald Duck.

themeparkpress.com/books/duck-daddy-jack-hannah.htm

The Studio Life of a Disney Legend

Eric Larson, one of Walt Disney's famed "Nine Old Men", went to work at the studio in 1933 and left in 1986. He knew everyone at Disney who was anyone, and he kept a diary of the personalities, the pranks, and the politics. This is his warm, witty story.

themeparkpress.com/books/50-years-mouse-house.htm

Advice for Living Happily Ever After

From *Snow White and the Seven Dwarfs* (1937) through *Big Hero 6* (2014), Jim Korkis takes you behind the scenes of 54 Disney animated films. Nearly eight decades of Disney, in a book not just packed with trivia, but with life lessons served up by Disney characters, loved and loathed alike.

themeparkpress.com/books/everything-learned-disney-animated-feature-films.htm